REGENERATION

REGENERATION

Being 'Born Again':
What it means
and
why it's necessary

John Charles Ryle

© Christian Focus Publications 2003

ISBN 1-85792-741-9
ISBN 978-1-85792-741-2

Published in 2003,
Reprinted 2007
in the
Christian Heritage Imprint
by
Christian Focus Publications Ltd.,
Geanies House, Fearn, Ross-shire,
IV20 1TW, Scotland, UK.

www.christianfocus.com

Cover design by Alister MacInnes

Printed and bound by
Nørhaven Paperback A/S, Denmark

Contents

'Sacraments must be used holily, and yet not to have the office of Christ added to them. Solely it is His office to sanctify and purge from sin. I take nothing from the sacraments, but honour them in all things, as they are worthy; howbeit not too much'

(Bishop Hooper, Reformer and Martyr, 1550).

REGENERATION

Reader

I wish to speak to you about regeneration, or being born again.

The subject is a most important one at any time. Those words of our Lord Jesus Christ to Nicodemus are very solemn, 'Except a man be born again, he cannot see the kingdom of God' (John 3:3). The world has gone through many changes since those words were spoken. Eighteen hundred years have passed away. Empires and kingdoms have risen and fallen. Great men and wise men have lived, laboured, written and died. But there stands the rule of the Lord Jesus unaltered and unchanged, and there it will stand, till heaven and earth shall pass away – 'Except a man be born again, he cannot see the kingdom of God.'

But the subject is one which is doubly important in the present day. Things have happened which have drawn special attention to it. Men's minds are full of it, and men's eyes are fixed on it. Regeneration is discussed in newspapers. Regeneration is talked of in private society. Regeneration is argued about in courts of law. Surely it is a time when every true Christian should examine himself upon the subject, and make sure that his views are sound. It is a time when we should not halt between two opinions. We should try to know what we hold. We should be ready to give a reason for our belief. When truth is assailed, those who love truth should grasp it more firmly than ever. Oh! for a greater spirit of decision throughout the law! Oh! for a more hearty determination to be always on the Lord's side!

Reader, I invite you to listen to me, while I try to bring this disputed question before you. I feel deeply that I can tell you nothing new. I know I can say nothing which has not been better said by better men than myself. But every additional witness may be of use in a disputed cause. And if I can only throw a little Scripture light on the subject of regeneration, and make it plain to plain readers of the Bible, I shall thank God, and be abundantly satisfied. What are the opinions of men to you or me? He that judgeth us is the Lord! One point has to be ascertained, and only one – 'What saith the Scripture of truth?'

Now I propose to attempt four things: firstly, to explain *what regeneration, or being born again means*; secondly, to show *the necessity of regeneration*; thirdly, to point out *the marks and evidences of regeneration*; fourthly, to answer *the objections most commonly raised against the view I hold.* If the Lord God shall enable me to make these four points clear to you, I believe I shall have done your soul a great service.

I

WHAT REGENERATION MEANS

Let me then first of all explain, *what regeneration, or being born again, means.*

Regeneration means, that change of heart and nature which a man goes through when he becomes a true Christian.

I think there can be no question that there is an immense difference among those who profess and call themselves Christians. Beyond all dispute there are always two classes in the outward Church – the class of those who are Christians in name and form only, and the class of those who are Christians in deed and in truth. All were not Israel who were called Israel, and all are not Christians who are called Christians. 'In the visible Church,' says an Article of the Church of England, 'the evil be ever mingled with the good.'

Some, as the Thirty-nine Articles say, are 'wicked and void of a lively faith': others, as another Article says, 'are made like the image of God's only begotten Son Jesus Christ, and walk religiously in good works.' Some worship God as a mere form, and some in spirit and in truth. Some give their hearts to God, and some give them to the world. Some believe the Bible and live as if they believed it: others do not. Some feel their sins and mourn over them: others do not. Some love Christ, trust in Him, and serve Him: others do not. In short, as Scripture says, some walk in the narrow way, some in the broad; some are the good fish of the gospel net, some are the bad; some are the wheat in Christ's field, and some are the tares.[1]

I think no man with his eyes open can fail to see all this, both in the Bible and in the world around him. Whatever he may think about the subject I am writing of, he cannot possibly deny that this difference exists.

Now what is the explanation of the difference? I answer, unhesitatingly, regeneration or being born again. I answer that true Christians are what they are, because they are regenerate, and formal Christians are what they are, because they are not. The heart of the Christian in deed has been changed. The heart of the Christian in name only has not been changed. The change of heart makes the whole difference.[2]

The change of heart is spoken of continually in the Bible, under various emblems and figures.

Ezekiel calls it 'a taking away the stony heart and a giving an heart of flesh'; 'a giving a new heart, and a putting within us a new spirit' (Ezek. 11:19; 36:26).

The Apostle John sometimes calls it being 'born of God'; sometimes being 'born again'; sometimes being 'born of the Spirit' (John 1:13; 3:3, 6).

The Apostle Peter in the Acts calls it 'repenting and being converted' (Acts 3:19).

The Epistle to the Romans speaks of it as a 'being alive from the dead' (Rom. 6:13).

The second Epistle to the Corinthians calls it 'being a new creature, old things having passed away, and all things become new' (2 Cor. 5:17).

The Epistle to the Ephesians speaks of it as a resurrection together with Christ, 'you hath he quickened who were dead in trespasses and sins' (Eph. 2:1) as 'a putting off the old man which is corrupt – being renewed in the spirit of our mind – and putting on the new man which after God is created in righteousness and true holiness' (Eph. 4:22, 24).

The Epistle to the Colossians calls it 'a putting off the old man with his deeds, and a putting on the new man which is renewed in knowledge after the image of him that created him' (Col. 3:9, 10).

The Epistle to Titus calls it 'the washing of regeneration and renewing of the Holy Ghost' (Titus 3:5).

The first Epistle of Peter speaks of it as 'a being called out of darkness into God's marvellous light' (1 Pet. 2:9). And the second Epistle as 'being made partakers of the divine nature' (2 Pet. 1:4).

The first Epistle of John calls it a 'passing from death to life' (1 John 3:14).

All these expressions come to the same thing in the end. They are all the same truth only viewed from different sides. And all have one and the same meaning. They describe a great radical change of heart and nature – a thorough alteration and transformation of the whole inner man, a participation in the resurrection life of Christ, or, to borrow the words of the Church Catechism, 'a death unto sin and a new birth unto righteousness'.[3]

This change of heart in a true Christian is so complete that no word could be chosen more fitting to express it than that word 'regeneration' or new birth. Doubtless it is no outward, bodily alteration, but undoubtedly it is an entire alteration of the inner man. It adds no new faculties to a man's mind, but it certainly gives an entirely new bent and bias to all his old ones. His will is so new, his taste so new, his opinions so new, his views of sin, the world, the Bible, and Christ so new, that he is to all intents and purposes a new man. The change seems to bring a new being into existence. It may well be called being *born again*.

This change is not always given to believers at the same time in their lives. Some are born again when they are infants, and seem, like Jeremiah and John the Baptist, filled with the Holy Ghost even from their mother's womb. Some few are born again in old age. The great majority of true Christians probably are born again after they grow up. A vast multitude of persons, it is to be feared, go down to the grave without having been born again at all.

This change of heart does not always begin in the same way in those who go through it after they have grown up. With some, like the Apostle Paul, and the jailer at Philippi, it is a sudden and violent change, attended with much distress of mind. With others, like Lydia of Thyatira, it is more gentle and gradual: their winter becomes spring almost without their knowing how. With some the change is brought about by the Spirit working through afflictions or providential visitations. With others, and probably the greater number of true Christians, the word of God preached, or written, is the means of effecting it.[4]

This change is one which no man can give to himself, nor yet to another. It would be as reasonable to expect the dead to raise themselves, or to require an artist to give a marble statue life. The sons of God are 'born not of blood, nor of the will of the flesh, nor of the will of man, but of God' (John 1:13). Sometimes the change is ascribed to God the Father, 'The God and Father of our Lord Jesus Christ... hath begotten us again unto a lively hope' (1 Pet. 1:3). Sometimes it is ascribed to God the Son, 'The Son quickeneth whom he will' (John 5:21). 'If ye know that he is righteous, ye know that every one that doeth righteousness is born of him' (1 John 2:29). Sometimes it is ascribed to the Spirit, and He in fact is the great agent by whom it is always effected, 'That which is born of the Spirit is spirit' (John 3:6). But man has no power to work the change. It is something far, far beyond his reach. 'The condition of man after the fall of Adam,' says the tenth Article, 'is such that he cannot turn and prepare himself by his own natural strength and good works, to faith and calling upon God.' No minister on earth can convey grace to any one of his congregation at his discretion. He may preach as truly and faithfully as Paul or Apollos: but God must 'give the increase' (1 Cor. 3:6). He may baptize with water in the name of the Trinity: but unless the Holy Ghost accompanies and blesses the ordinance, there is no death unto sin, and no new birth unto righteousness. Jesus alone, the great Head of the Church, can baptize with the Holy Ghost. Blessed and happy are they who have the inward baptism as well as the outward.[5]

Reader, I lay before you the foregoing account of regeneration. I say it is that change of heart which is the distinguishing mark of a true Christian man, the invariable companion of a justifying faith in Christ, the inseparable consequence of vital union with Him, and the root and beginning of inward sanctification. I ask you to ponder it well before you go any further. It is of the utmost importance that your views should be clear upon this point – *what regeneration really is.*

I know well that many will not allow that regeneration is what I have described it to be. They will think the statement I have made, by way of definition, much too strong. Some hold that regeneration only means admission into a state of ecclesiastical privileges – being made a member of the Church – but does not mean a change of heart. Some tell us that a regenerate man has a certain power within him which enables him to repent and believe if he thinks fit, but that he still needs a further change in order to make him a true Christian. Some say there is a difference between regeneration and being born again. Others say there is a difference between being born again and conversion.

To all this I have one simple reply, and that is, I can find no such regeneration spoken of anywhere in the Bible. A regeneration which only means admission into a state of ecclesiastical privilege may be ancient and primitive for anything I know. But something more than this is wanted. A few plain texts of Scripture are needed; and these texts have yet to be found. Such a notion of regeneration is utterly inconsistent with that which St. John gives us in his first Epistle. It renders it necessary to invent the awkward theory that there are two regenerations, and is thus eminently calculated to confuse the minds of unlearned people, and introduce false doctrine. It is a notion which seems not to answer to the solemnity with which our Lord introduces the subject to Nicodemus. When He said, 'Verily, verily, except a man be born again, he cannot see the kingdom of God,' did He only mean, except a man be admitted to a state of ecclesiastical privilege? Surely He meant more than this. Such a regeneration a man might have, like Simon Magus, and yet never be saved. Such a regeneration he might never have, like the penitent thief, and yet see the kingdom of God. Surely he must have meant a change of heart. As to the notion that there is any distinction between being regenerate and being born again, it is one which will not bear examination. It is the general opinion of all who know Greek, that the two expressions mean one and the same thing.

To me indeed there seems to be much confusion of ideas, and indistinctness of apprehension in men's minds on this simple point, what regeneration really is – and all arising from not simply adhering to the word of God. That a man is admitted into a state of great privilege, when he is made a member of a pure Church of Christ, I do not for an instant deny. That he is in a far better and more advantageous position for his soul, than if he did not belong to the Church, I make no question. That a wide door is set open before his soul, which is not set before the poor heathen, I can most clearly see. But I do not see that the Bible ever calls this regeneration. And I cannot find a single text in Scripture which warrants the assumption that it is so. It is very important in theology to distinguish things that differ. Church privileges are one thing. Regeneration is another. I, for one, dare not confound them.[6]

I am quite aware that great and good men have clung to that low view of regeneration to which I have adverted.[7] But when a doctrine of the everlasting Gospel is at stake, I can call no man master. The words of the old philosopher are never to be forgotten, 'I love Plato, I love Socrates, but I love truth better than either.' I cannot help remarking that those who hold the view that there are two regenerations, can bring forward no text in proof of it. I firmly believe that no plain reader of the Bible only, would ever find this view there for himself, and that goes very far to make me suspect it is an idea of man's invention. The only regeneration that I can see in Scripture is, not a change of *state*, but a change of *heart*. That is the view, I once more assert, which the Church Catechism takes, when it speaks of the 'death unto sin and new birth unto righteousness', and on that view I take my stand.

Reader, the doctrine before you is one of vital importance. This is no matter of names, and words, and forms, about which I am writing, and you are reading. It is a thing that you and I must feel and know by experience, each for himself, if we are to be saved. Try, I beseech you, to become acquainted with it. Let not the din and smoke of controversy draw off your attention from your own heart. Is that heart changed? Alas! it is poor work to wrangle, and argue, and dispute about regeneration, if after all we know nothing about it within.

Reader, regeneration, or new birth, is the distinguishing mark of every true Christian. Now just consider what I say. Are you regenerate, or are you not?

2

THE NECESSITY FOR
REGENERATION

Let me show you, in the second place, *the necessity there is for our being regenerate, or born again.*

That there is such a necessity is most plain from our Lord Jesus Christ's words in the third chapter of St. John's Gospel. Nothing can be more clear and positive than His language to Nicodemus, 'Except a man be born again he cannot see the kingdom of God.' 'Marvel not that I said unto thee, ye must be born again' (John 3:3, 7).

The reason of this necessity is the exceeding sinfulness and corruption of our natural hearts. The words of St. Paul to the Corinthians are literally accurate, 'The natural man receiveth not the things of the Spirit of God, for they are foolishness unto him' (1 Cor. 2:14). Just as rivers flow downwards, and sparks fly upwards, and stones fall to the ground, so does man's heart naturally incline to what is evil. We love our soul's enemies, we dislike our soul's friends. We call good evil, and we call evil good. We take pleasure in Christ. We not only commit sin, but we also love sin. We not only need to be cleansed from the guilt of sin, but we also need to be delivered from its power. The natural tone, bias, and current of our minds must be completely altered. The image of God, which sin has blotted out, must be restored. The disorder and confusion which reigns within us must be put down. The first things must no longer be last, and the last first. The Spirit must let in the light on our hearts, put everything in its right place, and create all things new.

It ought always to be remembered that there are two distinct things which the Lord Jesus Christ does for every sinner whom He undertakes to save. He washes him from his sins in His own blood, and gives him a free pardon: this is his justification. He puts the Holy Spirit into his heart, and makes him an entirely new man: this is his regeneration.

The two things are both absolutely necessary to salvation. The change of heart is as necessary as the pardon; and the pardon is as necessary as the change. Without the pardon we have no right or title to heaven. Without the change we should not be meet and ready to enjoy heaven, even if we got there.

The two things are never separate. They are never found apart. Every justified man is also a regenerate man, and every regenerate man is also a justified man. When the Lord Jesus Christ gives a man remission of sins, He also gives him repentance. When He grants peace with God, he also grants power to become a son of God. There are two great standing maxims of the glorious Gospel, which ought never to be forgotten. One is, 'He that believeth not shall be damned' (Mark 16:16). The other is, 'If any man have not the Spirit of Christ, he is none of his' (Rom. 8:9).

Reader, the man who denies the universal necessity of regeneration can know very little of the heart's corruption. He is blind indeed who fancies that pardon is all we want in order to get to heaven, and does not see that pardon without a change of heart would be a useless gift. Blessed be God that both are freely offered to us in Christ's Gospel, and that Jesus is able and willing to give the one as well as the other.

Surely you must be aware that the vast majority of people in the world *see nothing, feel nothing, and know nothing in religion as they ought*. How and why is this, is not the present question. I only put it to your conscience: Is it not the fact?

Tell them of the sinfulness of many things which they are doing continually; and what is generally the reply? 'They see no harm.'

Tell them of the awful peril in which their souls are, of the shortness of time, the nearness of eternity, the uncertainty of life, the reality of judgment. They feel no danger.

Tell them of their need of a Saviour – mighty, loving, and divine, and of the impossibility of being saved from hell except by faith in Him. It all falls flat and dead on their ears. They see no such great barrier between themselves and heaven.

Tell them of holiness, and the high standard of living which the Bible requires. They cannot comprehend the need of such strictness. They see no use in being so very good.

There are thousands and tens of thousands of such people on every side of us. They will hear these things all their lives. They will even attend the ministry of the most striking preachers, and listen to the most powerful appeals to their consciences. And yet when you come to visit them on their deathbeds, they are like men and women who never heard these things at all. They know nothing of the leading doctrines of the Gospel by experience. They can render no reason whatever of their own hope.

And why and wherefore is all this? What is the explanation, what is the cause of such a state of things? It all comes from this, that man naturally has no sense of spiritual things. In vain the sun of righteousness shines before him: the eyes of his soul are blind, and cannot see it. In vain the music of Christ's invitations sounds around him: the ears of his soul are deaf, and cannot hear it. In vain the wrath of God against sin is set forth: the perceptions of his soul are stopped up – like the sleeping traveller, he does not perceive the coming storm. In vain the bread and water of life are offered to him; his soul is neither hungry for the one, nor thirsty for the other. In vain he is advised to flee to the great Physician: his soul is unconscious of its disease; why should he go? In vain you put a price into his hand to buy wisdom: the mind of his soul wanders, he is like the lunatic, who calls straws a crown and dust diamonds – he says, 'I am rich and increased with goods, and have need of nothing.' Ah! Reader, there is nothing so sad as the utter corruption of our nature. There is nothing so painful as the anatomy of a dead soul.

Now what does such a man need? He needs to be born again and made a new creature. He needs a complete putting off the old man, and a complete putting on the new. We do not live our natural life till we are born into the world, and we do not live our spiritual life till we are born of the Spirit.

But, reader, you must furthermore be aware that the vast majority of people *are utterly unfit to enjoy heaven in their present state*. I lay it before you as a great fact. Is it not so?

Look at the masses of men and women gathered together in our cities and towns, and observe them well. They are all dying creatures – all immortal beings – all going to the judgment seat of Christ – all certain to live for ever in heaven or in hell. But where is the slightest evidence that most of them are in the least degree meet and ready for heaven?

Look at the greater part of those who are called Christians, in every parish throughout the land. Take any parish you please, in town or country. Take that which you know best. What are the tastes and pleasures of the majority of people who live there? What do they like best, when they have a choice? What do they enjoy most, when they can have their own way? Observe the manner in which they spend their Sundays. Mark how little delight they seem to feel in the Bible and prayer. Take notice of the low and earthly notions of pleasure and happiness, which everywhere prevail, among young and old, among rich and poor. Mark well these things, and then think quietly over this question – 'What would these people do in heaven?'

You and I, it may be said, know little about heaven. Our notions of heaven may be very dim and indistinct. But at all events, I suppose we are agreed in thinking that heaven is a very holy place – that God is there – and Christ is there – and saints and angels are there – that sin is not there in any shape – and that nothing is said, thought, or done, which God does not like. Only let this be granted, and then I think there can be no doubt the great majority of people around us are as little fit for heaven as a bird for swimming beneath the sea, or a fish for living upon dry land.[1]

And what is it that they need in order to make them fit to enjoy heaven? They need to be regenerated and born again. It is not a little changing and outward amendment that they require. It is not merely the putting a restraint on raging passions, and the quieting of unruly affections. All this is not enough. Old age – the want of opportunity for indulgence – the fear of man may produce all this. The tiger is still a tiger even when he is chained, and the serpent is still a serpent even when he lies motionless and coiled up. The alteration needed is far greater and deeper. They must every one have a new nature put within them. They must every one be made new creatures. The fountain head must be purified. The root must be set right. Each one wants a new heart and a new will. The change required is not that of the snake, when he casts his skin, and yet remains a reptile still. It is the change of the caterpillar when he dies and his crawling life ceases; but from his body rises the butterfly – a new animal with a new nature.

All this, and nothing less, is required. Well says the Homily of Good Works, 'they be as much dead to God that lack faith, as those are to the world that lack souls.'

The plain truth is, the vast proportion of professing Christians in the world have nothing whatever of Christianity except the name. The reality of Christianity, the graces, the experience, the faith, the hopes, the life, the conflict, the tastes, the hungering and thirsting after righteousness – all these are things of which they know nothing at all. They need to be converted as truly as any among the Gentiles to whom Paul preached, and to be turned from idols and renewed in the spirit of their minds as really if not as literally. And one main part of the message which should be continually delivered to the greater portion of every congregation on earth is this – 'Ye must be born again.' I write this down deliberately. I know it will sound dreadful and uncharitable in many ears. But I ask any one to take the New Testament in his hand and see what it says is Christianity, and compare that with the ways of professing Christians, and then deny the truth of what I have written, if he can.

And now let every one who reads this paper remember this grand principle of Scriptural religion, 'No salvation without regeneration – no spiritual life without a new birth – no heaven without a new heart.'

Think not for a moment that the subject of this tract is a mere matter of controversy, an empty question for learned men to argue about, but not one that concerns you. Away with such an idea for ever! It concerns you deeply. It touches your own eternal interests. It is a thing that you must know for yourself, feel for yourself, and experience for yourself, if you would ever be saved. No soul of man, woman or child, will enter heaven without having been born again.[2]

And think not for one moment that this regeneration is a change which people may go through after they are dead, though they never went through it while they were alive. Away with such a notion for ever. Now or never is the only time to be saved. Now, in this world of toil and labour – or money-getting and business – now you must be prepared for heaven; if you are ever to be prepared at all. Now is the only time to be justified, now the only time to be sanctified, and now the only time to be born again. So sure as the Bible is true, the man who dies without these three things will only rise again at the last day to be lost for ever.

You may be saved and reach heaven without many things which men reckon of great importance – without riches, without learning, without books, without worldly comforts, without health, without house, without land, without friends; but without regeneration you will never be saved at all. Without your natural birth you would never have lived and moved and read this tract on earth: without a new birth you will never live and move in heaven. I bless God that the saints in glory will be a multitude that no man can number. I comfort myself with the thought that after all there will be 'much people' in heaven. But this I know and am persuaded of from God's word, that of all who reach heaven there will not be one single individual who has not been born again.[3]

'Are you born again?' I say to every one whose eye is upon this page. Once more I repeat what I have already said, 'no salvation without a new birth.'

3

THE MARKS OF
REGENERATION

Let me in the third place point out *the marks of being regenerate, or born again.*

It is a most important thing to have clear and distinct views on this part of the subject we are considering. You have seen what regeneration is, and why it is necessary to salvation. The next step is to find out the signs and evidences by which a man may know whether he is born again or not – whether his heart has been changed by the Holy Spirit, or whether his change is yet to come.

Now these signs and evidences are laid down plainly for us in Scripture. God has not left us in ignorance on this point. He foresaw how some would torture themselves with doubts and questionings, and would never believe it was well with their souls. He foresaw how others would take it for granted they were regenerate who had no right to do so at all. He has therefore mercifully provided us with a test and gauge of our spiritual condition in the first Epistle general of St. John. There He has written for our learning what the regenerate man is, and what the regenerate man does – his ways, his habits, his manner of life, his faith, his experience. Every one who wishes to possess the key to a right understanding of this subject should thoroughly study this first Epistle of St. John.

Reader, I invite your particular attention to these marks and evidences of regeneration, while I try to set them before you in order. Forget everything else in this tract, if you will, but do not forget this part of it. I might easily mention other evidences besides those I am about to mention. But I will not do so. I would rather confine myself to the first Epistle of St. John, because of the peculiar explicitness of its statements about the man that is born of God. He that hath an ear let him hear what the beloved Apostle says about the marks of regeneration.

First of all, St. John says, 'Whosoever is born of God doth not commit sin'; and again, 'Whosoever is born of God sinneth not' (1 John 3:9; 5:18).

A regenerate man *does not commit sin as a habit*. He no longer sins with his heart, and will, and whole inclination, as an unregenerate man does. There was probably a time when he did not think whether his actions were sinful or not, and never felt grieved after doing evil. There was no quarrel between him and sin – they were friends. Now he hates sin, flees from it, fights against it, counts it his greatest plague, groans under the burden of its presence, mourns when he falls under its influence, and longs to be delivered from it altogether. In one word, sin no longer pleases him, nor is even a matter of indifference: it has become the abominable thing which he hates. He cannot prevent it dwelling within him. 'If he said he had no sin, there would be no truth in him' (1 John 1:8); but he can say that he cordially abhors it, and the great desire of his soul is not to commit sin at all. He cannot prevent bad thoughts arising within him, and shortcomings, omissions and defects appearing both in his words and actions. He knows, as St. James says, that 'in many things we offend all' (James 3:2). But he can say truly, and as in the sight of God, that these things are a daily grief and sorrow to him, and that his whole nature does not consent unto them, as that of the unregenerate man does.

Reader, I place this mark before you. What would the Apostle say about you, Are you born of God?[1]

Secondly, St. John says, 'Whosoever believeth that Jesus is the Christ is born of God (1 John 5:1).

A regenerate man believes that Jesus Christ is the only Saviour by whom his soul can be pardoned and redeemed, that He is the divine person appointed and anointed by God the Father for this very purpose, and that beside Him there is no Saviour at all. In himself he sees nothing but unworthiness, but in Christ he sees ground for the fullest confidence, and trusting in Him he believes that his sins are all forgiven and his iniquities all put away. He believes that for the sake of Christ's unfinished work and death upon the cross he is reckoned righteous in God's sight, and may look forward to death and judgment without alarm.

He may have his fears and doubts. He may sometimes tell you he feels as if he had no faith at all. But ask him whether he is willing to trust in anything instead of Christ, and see what he will say. Ask him whether he will rest his hopes of eternal life on his own goodness, his own amendments, his prayers, his minister, his doings in Church and out of Church, either in whole or in part, and see what he will reply. Ask him whether he will give up Christ, and place his confidence in any other way of salvation. Depend upon it, he would say, that though he does feel weak and bad, he would not give up Christ for all the world. Depend upon it, he would say he found a preciousness in Christ, a suitableness to his own soul in Christ that he found nowhere else, and that he must cling to Him.

Reader, I place this mark also before you. What would the Apostle say about you! Are you born of God?

Thirdly, St. John says, 'Every one that doeth righteousness is born of Him' (1 John 2:29).

The regenerate man is a holy man. He endeavours to live according to God's will, to do the things that please God, to avoid the things that God hates. His aim and desire is to love God with heart, and soul, and mind, and strength, and to love his neighbour as himself. His wish is to be continually looking to Christ as his example as well as his Saviour, and to show himself Christ's friend by doing whatsoever Christ commands. No doubt he is not perfect. None will tell you that sooner than himself. He groans under the burden of indwelling corruption, cleaving to him. He finds an evil principle within him constantly warring against grace, and trying to draw him away from God. But he does not consent to it, though he cannot prevent its presence. In spite of all shortcomings, the average bent and bias of his way is holy, his doings holy, his tastes holy, and his habits holy. In spite of all his swerving and turning aside, like a ship beating up against a contrary wind, the general course of his life is in one direction, toward God and for God. And though he may sometimes feel so low, that he questions whether he is a Christian at all, in his calmer moments he will generally be able to say with old John Newton, 'I am not what I ought to be, I am not what I want to be, I am not what I hope to be in another world, but still I am not what I once used to be, and by the grace of God I am what I am.'[2]

Reader, I place this mark also before you. What would the Apostle say about you? Are you born of God?

Fourthly, St. John says, 'We know that we have passed from death unto life, because we love the brethren' (1 John 3:14).

A regenerate man *has a special love for all true disciples of Christ*. Like his Father in heaven he loves all men with a great general love, but he has a special love for them who are of one mind with himself. Like his Lord and Saviour, he loves the worst of sinners and could weep over them, but he has a peculiar love for those who are believers. He is never so much at home as when he is in their company. He is never so happy as when he is among the saints and the excellent of the earth. Others may value learning, or cleverness, or agreeableness, or riches, or rank, in the society they choose. The regenerate man values grace. Those who have most grace and are most like Christ are those he loves most. He feels that they are members of the same family with himself, his brethren, his sisters, children of the same Father. He feels that they are fellow soldiers, fighting under the same captain, warring against the same enemy. He feels that they are his fellow-travellers, journeying along the same road, tried by the same difficulties, and soon about to rest with him in the same eternal home. He understands them, and they understand him. There is a kind of spiritual freemasonry between them. He and they may be very different in many ways, in rank, in station, in wealth. What matter? They are Jesus Christ's people.

They are his Father's sons and daughters. Then he cannot help loving them.[3]

Reader, I place this mark also before you. What would the Apostle say about you? Are you born of God?

Fifthly, St. John says, 'Whatsoever is born of God overcometh the world' (1 John 5:4).

A regenerate man *does not make the world's opinion his rule of right and wrong*. He does not mind going against the stream of the world's ways, notions, and customs. 'What will men say?' is no longer a turning point with him. He overcomes the love of the world. He finds no pleasure in things which most around him call happiness. He cannot enjoy their enjoyments: they weary him: they appear to him vain, unprofitable, and unworthy an immortal being. He overcomes the fear of the world. He is content to do many things which all around him think unnecessary, to say the least. They blame him: it does not move him. They ridicule him: he does not give way. He loves the praise of God more than the praise of man. He fears offending Him more than giving offence to man. He has counted the cost. He has taken his stand. It is a small thing with him now whether he is blamed or praised. His eye is upon Him that is invisible. Him he is resolved to follow whithersoever he goeth. It may be necessary in this following to come out from the world and be separate. The regenerate man will not shrink from doing so.

Tell him that he is unlike other people, that his views are not the views of society generally, and that he is making himself singular and peculiar. You will not shake him. He is no longer the servant of fashion and custom. To please the world is quite a secondary consideration with him. His first aim is to please God.

Reader, I place this mark also before you. What would the Apostle say about you? Are you born of God?

Sixthly, St. John says, 'he that is begotten of God keepeth himself' (1 John 5:18).

A regenerate man is *very careful of his own soul*. He endeavours not only to keep clear of sin, but also to keep clear of everything which may lead to it. He is careful about the company he keeps. He feels that evil communications corrupt the heart, and that evil is far more catching than good, just as disease is more infectious than health. He is careful about the employment of his time; his chief desire about it is to spend it profitably. He is careful about the books he reads: he fears getting his mind poisoned by mischievous writing. He is careful about the friendships he forms: it is not enough for him that people are kind and amiable and good natured. All this is very well; but will they do good to his soul? He is careful over his own daily habits and behaviour: he tries to recollect that his own heart is deceitful, that the world is full of wickedness, that the devil is always labouring to do him harm, and therefore he would fain be always on his guard. He desires to live like a soldier in an enemy's country, to wear his armour continually, and to be prepared for temptation. He finds by experience that his soul is ever among enemies, and he studies to be a watchful, humble, prayerful man.

Reader, I place this mark also before you. What would the Apostle say of you? Are you born of God?

Such are the six great marks of regeneration, which God has given for our learning. Let every one who has gone so far with me read them over with attention, and lay them to heart. I believe they were written with a view to settle the great question of the present day, and intended to prevent disputes. Once more then I ask the reader to mark and consider them.[4]

I know there is a vast difference in the depth and distinctness of these marks among those who are regenerate. In some people they are faint, dim, feeble and hardly to be discerned. You almost need a microscope to make them out. In others they are bold, sharp, clear, plain and unmistakable, so that he who runs may read them. Some of these marks are more visible in some people, and others are more visible in others. It seldom happens that all are equally manifest in one and the same soul. All this I am quite ready to allow.

But still, after every allowance, here we find boldly painted the six marks of being born of God. Here are certain positive things laid down by St. John as parts of the regenerate man's character, as plainly and distinctly as the features of a man's face.

Here is an inspired Apostle writing one of the last general Epistles to the Church of Christ, telling us that a man born of God does not commit sin, believes that Jesus is the Christ, doeth righteousness, loves the brethren, overcomes the world, and keepeth himself. And more than once in the very same Epistle when these marks are mentioned the Apostle tells us that he who has not this or that mark is 'not of God'. I ask the reader to observe all this.

Now what shall we say to these things? What they can say who hold that regeneration is only an admission to outward Church privileges, I am sure I do not know. For myself I say boldly I can only come to one conclusion. That conclusion is, that those persons only are regenerate who have these six marks about them, and that all men and women who have not these marks are not regenerate, are not born again.[5]

Reader, have you these marks? I know not what your opinions may be on this much disputed subject of regeneration. I know not on which side you may rank yourself. But once for all I warn you, if you find nothing in yourself answering to the marks I have been speaking of, you have reason indeed to be afraid. Without these marks it is vain to fancy you are scripturally regenerate. The witness of the Apostle John is clear and express that you are not. There must be a certain family likeness between God and His children. Without it you are none of His. There must be some visible evidence of the Spirit being within you, as plain as the stamp upon gold and silver, however small. Without this evidence you are only boasting of a false gift. Show me thy faith without thy works, said the Apostle James, when he wrote against those who were content with a dead faith. Show me thy regeneration without its fruits, is an argument that ought to be pressed home on many a conscience in the present day.

Reader, if you have not these marks, awake to a sense of your danger. Arise from your sleep of indifference and unconcern. Know the immense peril of hell and eternal misery in which you stand. Begin to use diligently every means by which God is ordinarily pleased to give grace to men's hearts, when they have not received it in their youth. Be diligent in hearing the Gospel preached. Be diligent in reading the Bible. Be diligent, above all, in prayer to the Lord Jesus Christ for the gift of the Holy Spirit.

If you take this course, I have every hope for you. None ever sought the Lord Jesus Christ in simplicity and sincerity, and sought in vain. Refuse to take this course, and continue as you are, and then I have little hope for you, and many fears. If the Bible be true, you are not yet born again. You will not use the most likely means to obtain this mighty blessing. What can I say but this, 'the Lord have mercy upon your soul?'[6]

Reader, if you have these marks I have been speaking of, be advised, and strive every year to make them more clear and plain. Let your repentance be a growing habit, your faith an increasing faith, your holiness a progressive holiness, your victory over the world a more decided victory, your love to the brethren a more hearty love, your watchfulness over yourself a more jealous watchfulness. Take this advice, and you will never repent it. This is the way to be useful and happy in your religion. This is the way to put to silence the opposition of the enemies of truth. Let others, if they will, have regeneration on their tongues, and nowhere else. Let it be your care to have it shining forth in your life, and to feel it in your heart.

4

ANSWERS TO
VARIOUS OBJECTIONS

And now, in the last place, let me endeavour *to
answer the objections most commonly made to the view
of regeneration which I have laid down.*

I know well that many professing Christians
object to the statements I have been making. It does
not surprise me, because I believe those statements
are Scriptural and true. True doctrine has always
had many enemies. Justification by faith has always
been bitterly assailed by some. The truth about
regeneration is continually assailed in like manner
by others. If Satan cannot prevent men being
professing Christians, he will try to fill their minds
with error, and so prevent their getting all the good
that Christianity was meant to do them.

I feel it a duty not to finish this tract without
attempting to offer a reply to some of these

objections. In so doing I must ask the readers patient attention. They are so often to be heard in this day, that all who love the truth should be armed against them, and prepared to give them a plain answer.

I dislike all controversy most heartily. But there are days and times when controversy is thrust upon us by circumstances, whether we like it or not. On such days, unhappily, we have fallen. And this being the case, it becomes every believer to know the reason of his own opinion, and to be prepared to meet those who try to pervert his mind.

The first great objection I will notice is this. Many hold that *regeneration is always given in baptism, and that we ought to look on every baptized person as born again.*

My main reply to this view is this, that it is entirely unsupported by the New Testament. It looks plausible, and sounds well at first, but it has no foundation. There is a fatal absence of texts in proof of it. Sixteen times at least the new birth is mentioned in the New Testament.[1]

'Regeneration' is a word used twice, but only once in the sense of a change of heart. 'Born again', 'Born of God', 'Begotten of God', are expressions used frequently. Once the word 'water' is joined with the words born of the Spirit. Once the word 'washing' is joined with regeneration. Twice believers are said to be born of the word of God, the word of truth. Never in any one text is it expressly said that we are born again by baptism, and that every baptized person is regenerate by virtue of his baptism. Never, I repeat. Men may search from the first of Matthew to the last chapter of Revelation, but a plain text connecting the new birth inseparably with baptism cannot be found.

But, furthermore, the reader must remember that we cannot say all baptized people are regenerate, without making out regeneration to be an entirely different thing from what it is described to us in Scripture. The view to which I am objecting finds acceptance with many, because it seems to exalt the sacrament of baptism. It would be well if such people would bear in mind that they cannot hold it without awfully depreciating and disparaging the holy doctrine of spiritual regeneration.

I ask any one whether it is not clear as daylight that multitudes of baptized people have not one single mark of being born of God, of all the six plain marks which St. John lays down. They do commit sin, and often with a high hand. They do not believe on Jesus for salvation, they are often utterly ignorant of saving faith. They do not live righteous and holy lives – often the very reverse. They do not love the brethren, they often quite dislike them. They do not overcome the world, they often serve it entirely. They do not keep themselves, they are often completely thoughtless about their souls. And are they then regenerate? Are they born of God? Would St. John say they were? Does he not lay down most broadly the doctrine that without these marks men are not born of God? Reader, it is a telling and striking fact that, much as St. John says in his first Epistle about regeneration, he never even mentions baptism.

The plain truth is, that there are two parts in baptism, the outward visible sign, and the inward spiritual grace, and that these two do not always go together. Water, we all know, is one part; a death unto sin, and a new birth unto righteousness, is the other part. But many are partakers of the outward sign, who are not partakers of the inward grace. Many receive the sprinkling of water, who never receive the new birth unto righteousness. Many are baptized with water, and born of water, who are not baptized with the Spirit, nor born of the Spirit. And as for saying that regeneration is always given in baptism, and that every baptized person is born again, it is an assertion that cannot be reconciled with Scripture, and is contrary to the judgment of many of the best English divines.[2]

This seems the lesson taught by St. Paul, when he says, 'He is not a Jew which is one outwardly, neither is that circumcision which is outward in the flesh. But he is a Jew which is one inwardly, and circumcision is that of the heart, in the spirit and not in the letter' (Rom. 2:28, 29). Circumcision was a sacrament to the Jews before Christ came, which filled the place of baptism to the Christian after Christ left the world. And yet Paul speaks of circumcision as if it might be received outwardly, without any grace or blessing to the receiver. Jeremiah does the same when he calls the house of Israel 'uncircumcised in the heart' (Jer. 9:26). Stephen does the same when he tells the Jews, 'they are uncircumcised in heart and ears' (Acts 7:51). And I believe the Apostle Paul would have us understand that just as circumcision might be received without profit, so also might baptism. I believe he would have said, 'He is not a Christian which is one outwardly, neither is that baptism which is outward in the flesh.' I know well that the reply to this argument will be, that circumcision was no sacrament, and was a mere form of admission into the Jewish Church, which in no case conveyed grace. But this reply will not avail any member of the Church of England. The words of the Homily of Common Prayer are distinct and clear, 'circumcision was a sacrament'. The Apostle Paul asserts broadly that it was a seal of the righteousness of faith. Once let it be granted that it was a sacrament, and there is no way of evading the Apostle's argument. Just as a Jew might be circumcised in flesh, and yet remain uncircumcised in heart, so may a Christian be baptized with water, and yet never receive the baptism of the Spirit. In the New Testament, as well as in the Old, the sign and the grace are often separated. The one may be had without the other.[3]

This seems the lesson we are meant to learn from the several accounts of baptism which we find in the New Testament. Glorious things are spoken in some of the Epistles of the privileges which accompany baptism, when rightly received. 'We are buried with Christ by baptism into death,' says Paul to the Romans (Rom. 6:4). 'Buried with Christ in baptism, wherein also ye are risen with him,' he says again to the Colossians (Col. 2:12). But no man, I think, can fairly examine the description of baptism which we have in the Acts, without seeing that baptism may be unworthily received by some, and that others may receive the death unto sin and new birth unto righteousness before they are baptized at all. In the case of Simon Magus there was baptism, but no regeneration. The words of the Apostle Peter are plain and express, 'Thou hast neither part nor lot in this matter, thy heart is not right in the sight of God, thou art in the gall of bitterness, and in the bond of iniquity' (Acts 8:21, 23). In the case of Cornelius and his friends it is equally clear that regeneration went before baptism. 'Can any man forbid water,' says Peter, 'that these should not be baptized who have received the Holy Ghost as well as we?' (Acts 10:47). Then let us add to this the striking fact that the Apostle Paul, when writing to the Corinthians, actually says, 'I thank God that I baptized none of you... Christ sent me not to baptize, but to preach the gospel' (1 Cor. 1:14-17). Is it possible to suppose he would ever have used this expression, if he held that baptism always conveyed regeneration? To my own mind it is utterly incredible. Last of all, let us remember the case of the penitent thief. If ever man was born of God, he was the man. None ever showed such striking evidences of regeneration. No child of Adam ever received such a strong assurance from the Lord's mouth of entering the kingdom of God, 'Today shalt thou be with me in paradise' (Luke 23:43). And yet we have not the slightest spark of evidence that this man was ever baptized at all.

I ask the reader to put together these Scriptural facts, and to allow them their due weight. I ask him to observe especially, that regeneration is frequently and constantly spoken of without the slightest allusion to baptism. I ask him to observe that in some texts the word of God is particularly named as the instrument of regeneration, and not baptism. I ask him to observe how a man may be regenerate before he is baptized, and how a man may be baptized and yet afterwards manifestly not be regenerate at all. And then I ask him how it is possible to avoid the conclusion that regeneration is not inseparably tied to baptism. It is the only conclusion I can draw, and I therefore say that the objection that all baptized people are regenerate is an objection without foundation, and cannot stand.[4]

The second objection I will notice is this. It is said, that *the view of regeneration I maintain is dishonouring to the sacrament of baptism, and that it makes baptism in the greater number of cases to be nothing at all.*

I utterly deny this charge. If I considered regeneration to be nothing more than a change of state, and an outward admission to Church privileges, I should think there was some truth in it. They are the men who dishonour baptism, to my mind, who say that baptism confers this mere outward change, and no more. It is at their door that this charge should lie.

For myself, I take a far higher view of the blessing connected with baptism. I believe with the Catechism of my own Church that it is a means whereby we receive inward and spiritual grace, when it is rightly received. And I believe with the Catechism that this grace is a death unto sin and a new birth unto righteousness, and nothing less. I do not see how our Church could possibly take a lower view than this, with such a plain text before us as that in the first Epistle of Peter, 'Baptism doth also now save us (not the putting away of the filth of the flesh, but the answer of a good conscience toward God), by the resurrection of Jesus Christ' (1 Peter 3:21). Of course I do not mean to say that the mere material element of water has any power to wash away sins. It can only wash us, as our Church service says, mystically and figuratively. It cannot wash us spiritually, or touch the soul. But I do mean to say that baptism, as an ordinance appointed by Christ Himself, is intended to convey to us the highest spiritual blessings, and that where it is used rightly, worthily, and with faith, we may confidently expect that the Lord Jesus Christ will meet and seal those blessings to our souls. And I do not for a moment hesitate to affirm that every man who has rightly and worthily received baptism is a regenerate man.[5]

But just as the Church Catechism most carefully abstains from saying that baptism is 'the means' whereby we receive a death unto sin and a new birth unto righteousness, so also must I abstain. It is one thing to call it '*a*' means of regeneration. It is quite another to call it '*the*' means. To call it '*the means*' would of course imply that there is no other way of being born again. To call it '*a means*' only implies that it is one way among several. The expression '*the means*' would tie regeneration inseparably to baptism. The expression '*a means*' seems to admit, that the outward sign of water, and the inward peace of new birth do not always go together, and that the person baptized may not receive baptism worthily, and may yet need to be born again of the word. This, I consider, is the true view to take. This is precisely suitable to the whole testimony of Scripture on the subject. And if to hold this is to hold views dishonourable to baptism, I must freely confess that the charge sits very lightly on my conscience. It is only saying what the Bible and the Catechism of my own Church say about it, and I need not therefore feel much ashamed.

It does not however follow, because baptism is not always accompanied by regeneration, that a baptized man who is not regenerate, has received no benefit from his baptism. I do not at all concede this. It is a common accusation which is brought against the views that I hold, but it is one of which I deny the truth. I believe that baptism always confers many outward privileges. It makes a man a member of the visible church of Christ. It gives him advantages and opportunities of which the heathen know nothing. It places him within reach of the bread of life. It opens to him a great door, which is shut to the heathen altogether. It gives him a lawful place in the congregation, and a right to the ministry of the word. These things no doubt are not regeneration. Thousands have no more sense of their value, than Esau had of the value of his birthright. But still the man who has them is in a far higher position than the heathen. He has far more light and far more responsibility, and if his talents are not improved, will find in the end that he has far more sin.

I cannot leave this part of the subject without quoting a passage from that admirable divine, Archbishop Usher, which appears to me to place the matter of baptismal privilege just where it ought to be placed. He says in his Body of Divinity: 'What is the advantage or benefit of baptism to the common Christian? The same as was the benefit of circumcision to the Jew outward (Rom. 2:28). There is a general grace of baptism which all the baptized partake of as a common favour; and that is their admission into the visible body of the Church; their matriculation and outward incorporation into the number of the worshippers of God by external communion. And so as circumcision was not only a seal of the righteousness which is by faith, but as an overplus, God appointed it to be a wall of separation between Jew and Gentile: so is baptism a badge of an outward member of the Church, a distinction from the common sort of the brethren. And God thereby seals a right upon the party baptized to His ordinances, that

He may use them as His privileges, and wait for an inward blessing by them. Yet this is but the porch, the shell, and outside. All that are outwardly received into the visible Church are not spiritually ingrafted into the mystical body of Christ. Baptism is attended upon always by that general grace, but not always by that special.' I feel I can add nothing to this statement. Nothing can be more unfair than the common objection, that we degrade the sacrament of baptism, because we will not allow that it always confers regeneration. I refuse to speak of baptism as if it were *everything* as many do. I do not however on that account maintain that it is *nothing* at all. I rather say that it is attended by great privileges in every case, and by the greatest spiritual blessings in some cases. And this in spite of all objections, I believe is the Scriptural view.

The third objection I will notice is this. It is said that *infants at any rate are always regenerated in baptism. They place no bar in the way of grace accompanying the outward sign of water. Therefore they must always receive baptism worthily, and always be born again.*

This is at first sight a very plausible objection, and much weight has been attached to it. I trust however to be enabled to show that there are very strong reasons against it and that when touched with the spear of calm scriptural examination, it is worth nothing at all.

Let me clear the way by reminding the reader that the salvation of children who die in infancy, is not the point to be considered. As to the souls of such children, I feel no doubt. I believe, with many sound divines, that all are saved who die in infancy, whether unbaptized or baptized. I would even hope well, in such a case of the infants of infidels and heathen. Others may think it right to say that baptism is absolutely necessary to salvation, and that all children who die unbaptized are damned. I shrink with horror from such a doctrine, and leave it to those who hold it, to defend it if they can. The point to be considered, is not the salvation of infants, but the precise effect of baptism upon them. I say all this, because some people seem to fancy that if we doubt whether all children who were baptized are regenerated, we must also doubt whether all children who die in infancy are saved. Once more let me remind the reader, these two are distinct questions.

Now the precise effect of baptism on infants is never once distinctly stated in the New Testament. There is no account of a child's baptism, and no description of the effect of baptism upon a child. No one, I think, can controvert this. Men may vary in their views of the subject, but it is perfectly certain that one single direct text about it cannot be brought forward, from the first verse of Matthew to the last of Revelation. All the conclusions that we arrive at on this point must be arrived at indirectly and in the way of inference. This, of itself, is a startling fact, but a fact that cannot be gainsayed. This alone might teach us to look on the assertion that all infants are born again in baptism with great suspicion. The assertion is one that involves such grave consequences, that we must have clear proofs from Scripture, before we receive it for truth. These proofs have never yet been given. To quote texts which show a connection between baptism and regeneration, or to talk about the Nicene Creed and one baptism for the remission of sins, decides nothing at all. That the grace of regeneration may, and in many cases does, accompany the baptism of an infant, I, for one, never think of disputing. But the question is, Does this grace always and invariably attend the baptism of every infant? I reply unhesitatingly, that it does not. I say so, because I cannot find a text that proves it. Without the evidence of scripture such a doctrine ought not to be received, and if a man is to be called a heretic for not receiving it, the supremacy of Scripture, as the rule of faith, is at an end.

I do not however wish the reader to be content with this negative kind of reasoning on the subject. I will go on to mention two or three other points which are worth considering, in forming an opinion about it. And I trust to be enabled to show that there are other grounds for rejecting the doctrine that all infants are in a matter of course regenerated in baptism, as well as the great fact already put forward, that there is not a word about it in the Bible.

Ought we not then to remember that no infant is meet and worthy in itself, to receive inward and spiritual grace in baptism? It is brought to baptism, a feeble, unconscious being, and doubtless places no bar wilfully in the way of God's blessing. But I cannot find proof that this alone makes it worthy. The absence of one thing does not necessarily involve the presence of another. The absence of wilful impediment does not constitute positive worthiness. It is born in sin. It is a child of wrath. It naturally deserves God's wrath and condemnation. To doubt this would be a denial of original sin, and Pelagianism of the worst kind. God's free and sovereign grace can make the infant worthy, and I make no question does make many an one worthy. But what warrant have we for saying that this grace is bestowed on all infants who are baptized indiscriminately? What warrant have we for broadly saying that the most High God, who has mercy on whom he will have mercy, and calls on those whom He will, does certainly call by His Spirit every single infant whom we present to Him at the font? We have no warrant, I unhesitatingly say, no warrant at all. I hope charitably about the souls of all infants, and I do so because of the largeness of the mercy and grace of God. I hope more strongly about some than I do about others, and I do so because of the exceeding freeness of God's promises to the seed of believers. But beyond this I dare not go. I have no Scripture to lead me, and in such matters I dare not travel in the dark.

Ought we not furthermore to remember that no infant possesses in itself any right or title to be baptized at all. It can only receive the outward sign of the sacrament, as the child of professing Christian parents. It is only as the seed and offspring of persons who are members of the Church, that it has any claim to be added to the visible Church of Christ, and receive a Christian name. Someone must present it. Someone must undertake to answer for it at the font. The witness of our own Church is worth observation on this point. The Catechism puts the question, 'Why are infants baptized?' and supplies an answer. That answer is not 'because they are worthy', nor yet 'because they put no bar in the way of grace'. It is simply, 'because they promise repentance and faith by their sureties.' This is a point far too much lost sight of.[6]

Now surely if an infant's right to baptism comes through its parents, it is not too much to say that it makes a great difference what kind of parents those parents are. It makes a great difference in the degree of confidence we must feel as to the exact blessing the child will receive. Are we to be told that faith and prayer have nothing whatever to do with the effect of the sacrament? Are we really to be told that it makes no matter at all what the parents are, that the child of the drunkard, and the child of the true believer in Christ – the child of the prayerless and the child of the praying – do all receive precisely the same benefit? Are we to give the parents in our congregations to understand that whatever may be the spirit and way in which they bring their infants to baptism, the effect is always the same – that in fact they may be ignorant, careless, despisers of means of grace, unholy, profane, but that their child shall get just the same inward blessing from baptism as the child of their neighbour who is a holy follower of Christ? Is this what we are to say?

I dare not say so, whatever others may do? I dare not say so, when I see how much the spiritual condition of children is said in Scripture to hinge and turn on the conduct of their parents, and how continually we see proof of it in the world around us. I cannot think that the faith and prayers of parents and sponsors have nothing to do with the full efficacy of baptism. I dare not say so, as a minister of the Church of England, when I look at the baptismal service of the Church. I observe that even in the special case of the private baptism of an infant – which is only allowable on an emergency, such as its being in a dying state – even then the minister is not to baptize without first calling upon God and prayer. And I observe that the public service of baptism makes prayer a most important part of the ordinance. The exhortations 'to pray, to call upon God the Father, to ask, to seek, to knock, to doubt not, to believe earnestly', are strikingly put forward before the infant is baptized. I cannot for a moment think that all these exhortations were a mere form, and in no way connected with the full blessing of the sacrament. To my mind they seem to imply that when the sacrament of baptism is received with contempt, we ought to doubt whether it really gives what it promises, and conveys what it signifies. I see hundreds and thousands of parents bringing their children to baptism in this contemptuous way, and when

I see this I must feel strong doubts whether their children are sure to get an inward blessing from the sacrament. I would not be misunderstood. I would not absolutely tie the grace of God to the faith and prayers of parents and sponsors, any more than I would tie it to the water. But as for saying that a baptism without a parent's faith and prayer, is just as efficacious as baptism with faith and prayer, I dare not do it.

Ought we not, above all, to be very careful that we do not admit the Romish doctrine of grace 'ex opere operato'. I mean by that, the doctrine that, if the form of an ordinance be gone through, the grace of God must necessarily accompany it.

Now I conceive that the objection I am contending against is this Romish doctrine of grace 'ex opere operato', in the barest and most naked form, and if there were no other reason against it but this, ought on this account to be strenuously resisted. Many will tell us that if there be only the sprinkling of water in the name of the Trinity, there is always regeneration; that in spite of utter ignorance, contempt, unbelief, and prayerlessness, on the part of all connected with the child, it is always born again, and always has the seed of eternal life placed in its heart. To my mind such a doctrine is positively awful. It seems insulting to God, calculated to foster the worst kind of superstition and formality, and the surest way to make parents neglect Scriptural training and prayer for their children. What need of it all if they are regenerated as a matter of course? That mere sprinkling with water in the name of the Trinity may make a valid baptism, I have no doubt, but it is quite another thing to say that it is necessarily regeneration.

I cannot say so, whatever others may think. At this rate our missionaries among the heathen are going on an entirely wrong system. No true Protestant missionary ever thinks of baptizing indiscriminately all the heathen children he can find. A Roman Catholic may do so perhaps. This is in fact the plan on which Xavier acted in India, and then boasted that he regenerated so many hundreds of souls every day. This is the plan which the Spaniards adopted in South America: they baptized their unhappy captives before they shot them, that they might make sure of their going to heaven. But no true Protestant missionary ever acts upon this system. And yet, if children have a right to baptism merely because they are children, and are all born again the moment they are baptized, who can doubt that our missionaries ought to spend a great part of their time in baptizing all the heathen children they can find? According to the view of my present objector, it would at once regenerate them. They put no bar in the way. But our missionaries do not do so, and it would be well for some persons to consider calmly why they do not.

For my part I cannot find any ground in Scripture for supposing that God has ever bound Himself to bless any ordinance of His, if the outward *form* of it only be used, without respect to the *manner* in which it is used. I cannot put my finger on a single ceremony in the Old or New Testament, in which the outward and formal performance by itself conveyed an inward and spiritual blessing. I find, on the contrary, the strongest language used to show that the very holiest ordinances are unprofitable if not rightly used. I hear God saying in the prophet Isaiah, 'I delight not in the blood of bullocks, incense is an abomination to me, your appointed feasts my soul hateth' (Isa. 1:11-14). I cannot think that God's mind is different on the subject of baptism from what it is on the subject of other ordinances. I believe that under the New Testament dispensation faith and the heart are more than ever needful in all our approaches to God, and that far more than the Jews we are called upon to worship God in spirit and truth. And this being the case, I cannot for a moment believe that the mere outward administration of the sacrament of baptism must, as a matter of course, convey a great inward and spiritual blessing. Surely, when Scripture is so perfectly silent on the subject, the positive language that is frequently used in the present day about the invariable effect of baptism cannot be justified. Surely the cautious language of old Hooker is far preferable, when he says, 'Sacraments are not physical but moral instruments of salvation, which unless we perform as the author of grace requireth, they are unprofitable; for all receive not the grace of God which receive the sacraments of his grace.'[7]

Reader, I recommend the foregoing argument to your calm consideration. The entire absence of all direct Scriptural evidence; the unwarrant-ableness of the assertion that God must necessarily give the Holy Spirit to every infant that is baptized; the unreasonableness of holding that a child's right to baptism is ordinarily through its parents, and yet that the faith and prayers of its parents are to go for nothing at all; the dangerous and painful consequences of admitting the doctrine of grace 'ex opere operato' – all these taken together make up a reason to my mind why the objection that all infants must, as a matter of course, be regenerated in baptism cannot stand.

The fourth objection I will notice is this. It is said that, *if we do not allow that all baptized persons are regenerate by virtue of their baptism, we are making the privileges of the Christian lower than those of the Jew.*

The argument of such an objector, if I understand it aright, runs as follows. The Jews were all called the children of God. If children of God, it follows that they must have been born of God. Therefore, all Jews were born of God. But if it be true, as I have been contending, that all Christians are not born of God, it would seem that I make out the Jew to be in a higher state of privilege than the Christian.

My reply to such an argument is, that it is built upon an assumption. It takes things for granted which I cannot allow as proved. It is, in short, a fallacy.

It takes for granted that people are called children of God in the Old Testament, in the same high and holy sense that they are in the New. Now this is just the point in the argument that I deny.

The Jews were called the children of God in the Old Testament because of their national privileges. They were a people chosen by God from among the nations of the earth, joined to Him by a special covenant, adopted as His own peculiar people, distinguished from all other families in the world by outward marks and ordinances, and by virtue of this national adoption they are frequently spoken of as God's children. But their sonship was a mere external sonship of national relation, and no more. It did not imply, as a necessary consequence, any inward change of heart whatever.

Believers and disciples of Christ, on the other hand, in the New Testament, are called children of God, because of their moral relation to Him, and in no other sense. They are the 'children of God by faith in Christ Jesus'. Because they are sons, 'God hath sent forth the Spirit of His Son into their hearts, crying, Abba Father' (Gal. 3:26; 4:6). The Father has called them by His Spirit, and made them children by adoption and grace. They are regarded as members of His dear Son's mystical body, and parts of His elect family. But their sonship is purely a sonship of moral relation. It implies something far more than Church membership, or outward union to a certain body. It implies a spiritual change of the inner man, a new creation in Christ Jesus, and a conformity to His image.

The sonship of the Jew did not necessarily involve any faith, love, grace or change of heart. That many a pious Jew had all these, and was truly born again, I have no doubt. That many an Israelite was a son of God by the election of grace, and a son by faith, as well as a son by national relation, I make no question. But the ground I maintain is, that to say all Jews were born again and regenerated by the Holy Ghost, merely because they were called children of God, is saying that which cannot be proved. Where is the text throughout the whole of the Old Testament, which says that every circumcised man was born again, and had a new heart? What can be more plain than the testimony of St. Paul, in the end of the second chapter of the Epistle to the Romans, that such was not the case at all?

There is an expression used by our Lord Jesus Christ, in one of His conversations with the Jews, which throws much light upon this point. He says in St. John's Gospel, 'If God were your Father, ye would love me' (John 8:42). Does not that sentence plainly mean that those to whom our Lord spoke were not children of God in the spiritual sense, however they might be in a national sense? 'All who are true children of my Father,' our Lord seems to say, 'love me. Ye do not love me: therefore ye are not my Father's sons.' A little further on we find a text which almost comes to the same thing. 'He that is of God heareth God's words: ye therefore hear them not, because ye are not of God' (John 8:47).

Another expression of our Lord Jesus Christ may also be quoted before leaving this part of the subject. He says to Nicodemus, in the well-known passage in the third chapter of John, 'Ye must be born again' (John 3:7). Now Nicodemus was a Jew. In a national sense he was one of the children of God. And yet Nicodemus is told that he needs regeneration, or new birth, and not one word is said to imply that, as a Jew, he had it already. What can be more clear than the inference? It is one thing to be a child of God nationally, as the Israelite was. It is quite another to be born again, and be a child of God spiritually, as every true believer is.

The plain truth is, that there is not a whit more ground for saying all Jews were born again, than for saying all Christians are born again. Circumcision and union with God's professing Church under the Old Testament, by no means involved a change of heart. Baptism and union with the Church of Christ under the New Testament by no means involve a change of heart either. The Jew had many privileges, much light, teaching ceremonies, good ordinances. The Christian has far more privileges, far clearer light, far better ordinances. But one thing is common to both Jew and Christian. In neither case does the possession of privileges carry with it regeneration.

Regeneration is no mere outward ecclesiastical change. Regeneration is the peculiar mark of true believers. Regeneration is the inseparable companion of saving faith. Now which dispensation is most calculated under God to produce saving faith, the gospel of Christ or the law of Moses? Which is most likely to turn men from sin to God, and bring them salvation? We all know the answer. We are all agreed in thinking that the full sunlight of that gospel which makes the way into the holiest manifest, is far more soul-saving and life-giving than that law which made nothing perfect, and was only a schoolmaster to bring unto Christ. And surely if this be the case, the objector's argument that we make the circumcised Jew better off than the baptized Christian, falls completely to the ground. It is not so at all. The privileges of the Christian's position are as much higher than the Jew's, as the Gospel is higher than the law.

The fifth objection I will notice is this. It is said *there is no reason why we should not suppose all children to be regenerated, and receive the gift of the Holy Ghost in baptism, because the grace of God may be quenched and lost by neglect, or lie dormant like seed in the heart, and in many cases never be put in exercise at all.*

My answer is that there is one very serious reason against such a view, and that is we read of no such a regeneration in the Bible. It is a view purely of man's invention. Once for all I must urge upon the reader the immense importance of cleaving to the written word of God in all discussions of spiritual things, and also of calling things in religion by their right names. Where do we find the slightest hint that there is such a thing as dormant grace, or an indwelling of the Holy Spirit which cannot be seen, or a new birth which produces no effect in the heart and life? I confidently assert that the general doctrine of Scripture is, that when grace exists in the soul it will show itself, that when a man has the Spirit, he will bring forth, more or less, the fruits of the Spirit, and that regeneration is attended by marks and evidences which cannot be mistaken.

Such a view as that of my present objector flatly contradicts the accounts given by Saint John, of the man born of God. 'He doth not commit sin; for his seed remaineth in him, and he cannot sin because he is born of God' (1 John 3:9). The presence of the seed of grace, he seems to argue, will of itself keep the man from sin. But as to a man having the seed of grace in him, and deliberately continuing in sin, he implies that it is an impossibility. It contradicts the account given by Saint Peter in his first Epistle, 'being born again, not of corruptible seed, but of incorruptible' (1 Peter 1:23). The seed of grace, he there seems to argue, cannot die, be wasted, or spoiled, as the present objector would make out. It contradicts the broad doctrine repeatedly laid down by our Lord Jesus Christ, 'by their fruits ye shall know them'. It shifts the evidence of grace from a man's life to a man's baptism. It contradicts the great first principle with which Saint John begins his first Epistle, 'if we say we have fellowship with Him and walk in darkness, we lie and do not the truth' (1 John 1:6). The walk and conversation of a man is there specially mentioned, as the grand test of union and friendship with God. Now surely all these contradictions are trifling things.

But furthermore this view of dormant grace throws the whole doctrine of the work of the Spirit into confusion. If all baptized people alike have within them grace and the Holy Spirit, whether holy or unholy, believers or unbelievers, it does really seem to make out that grace and the Holy Spirit are nothing at all. If all baptized persons alike possess the Holy Ghost in their hearts, and the only difference among them is, that some think fit to make use of Him and some do not, it does appear to my apprehension that the third Person of the Blessed Trinity is placed in the position of a servant in the hands of a mere mortal, and that the whole work of salvation is completely put within the wicked man's own free will and power. I shrink from so dishonouring a view. I shrink from saying that people can be at the same time dead unto sin and yet living in sin, born again unto righteousness and living in unrighteousness, having the Spirit and yet doing the works of the flesh, children of God and yet children of the devil, new creatures and new men and yet manifestly by their actions cleaving to the ways of the old man. Yet all these are consequences that flow from admitting the doctrine of dormant grace.

Moreover this view is not borne out by experience and facts. If the thing were true there surely ought to be some distinguishable difference between infants who have been baptized and infants who have not. Surely there ought to be some greater response to injunctions to cease from evil, some greater readiness to learn to do well, some greater power of resisting the devil, and choosing that which is good in the baptized child, if baptism always and invariably implants a seed of grace. Yet will any one undertake to go into an infant school in some densely populated districts of London, and point out, after examining the school, who are the baptized children and who are not? I put a strong case in saying this. But I maintain, if the objector's view be grounded on truth, that in the beginning of a baptized child's life, this seed of grace ought to be seen. Surely every honest man must confess that in the case of great proportions of baptized children, not the slightest traces of this seed appear.

Moreover, this view is entirely unsupported by Scripture. Texts no doubt are brought forward on its behalf, but all will prove on enquiry to be misapplied, and taken out of their legitimate sense. Such texts as these 'stir up the gift of God that is in thee, neglect not the gift that is in thee, that good thing which was committed unto thee keep, keep that which is committed to thy trust' (2 Tim. 1:6; 1 Tim. 4:14; 2 Tim. 1:14; 1 Tim. 6:20) are often brought forward. But unfortunately they are every one purely ministerial, and refer to some special gift conferred on Timothy for ministerial purposes. 'Quench not the Spirit' (1 Thess. 5:19), is thought by many to refer to the ministerial gifts of others, and the verse following 'despise not prophesying' rather favours that interpretation. But we are not obliged to resort to such an explanation. We have only to observe that the exhortation was addressed to men whose faith, hope, love and election of God were known to Saint Paul, and then we see that it is an injunction specially addressed to true believers, and like 'grieve not the Spirit' in Ephesians, a most useful injunction for true believers to remember.

In saying all this, I am anxious not to be misunderstood. I am ready to make every allowance for the weakness of grace in a child. I feel strongly that we must not be too hasty in deciding whether a child is regenerate or not, and especially so, in the case of a child of a believer. It is vain to expect the same strong evidences from one whose faculties are all weak and mind unformed, as we expect to see in one grown up. But I say, unhesitatingly, when a child becomes old enough to know good and evil, and to be accountable for his actions, we must then begin to look for the marks of regeneration. And if those marks are not to be found even in the feeblest form, if there is no inclination whatever towards what is good, and no struggle whatever against what is evil, I know not how we can avoid the Scriptural conclusion, that the child is not yet regenerate, and must yet be born again. Well says the wisest of men, 'Even a child is known by his doings, whether his work is pure, and whether it be right' (Prov. 20:11).

I would have all young people continually reminded of their baptism, and I do not think they are sufficiently reminded of it in the present day. I would have them reminded of the promises and vows that were made for them, and of the privileges that wer⁓ sealed to them, if they will only put in their claim. But I think they should also be plainly told to examine themselves, and see what they know of the fruits of the Spirit. And I think they ought to be plainly warned that their baptism avails them nothing if they are not new creatures and have not a faith that works by love and purifies their hearts; that the life is the grand test of character, and that if no grace whatever appears in their lives, they have no grace within. Like the professedly Christian woman spoken of by Paul, who 'liveth in pleasure', they are dead, and need to be made alive again (1 Tim. 5:6); like those evil members of the Church described by Jude, they 'have not the Spirit' (Jude 19); and except they be born again, they will one day hear those solemn words, 'I never knew you', in spite of their baptism* (Matt. 7:23).[8]

Reader, I leave these thoughts also for your consideration. Beware of taking a low and degrading view of the grace of regeneration. Depend upon it, regeneration is not that small thing which many seem determined to make it. Depend upon it, it is not a thing which a man may possess, and yet others never be aware of it, never see it, never observe it in his life. Depend upon it, the grace of regeneration is a mighty, active, working, leavening principle, and when it cannot be seen, we have no right to say it exists. When we can understand how light can be unseen, and wind not felt, then perhaps we may understand how a man may be born again of the Spirit, and yet his new birth be neither known nor observed.

Once grant that all baptized people are born again, and one of two consequences must necessarily follow. Either you must believe that to be born again does not mean what the Bible says it does mean; or else you must believe that the marks of regeneration are not necessary in order to prove its existence. For myself I dare not hold either consequence. I hope charitably about all infants so long as they are infants. I am even more disposed to make allowance for much waywardness and infirmity in them than many are. But when a child has come to years of discretion, I only see one principle by which he can be tested. I say that he only is regenerate who has the marks of regeneration. 'If ye were Abraham's children, ye would do the works of Abraham' (John 8:39) was our Lord's teaching to the Jews; 'As many as are led by the Spirit of God, they,' and they only, 'are the sons of God' (Rom. 8:14) must be the doctrine of Christians.

The sixth and last objection I propose to notice is one that seems more weighty to some minds than many, and I shall therefore be excused if I answer it at greater length than any of the preceding ones. It is said by many *that the Church of England holds that all infants are invariably regenerated and born again in baptism*; that the words of her baptismal service – 'Seeing now that this child is regenerate, we yield thee hearty thanks that it hath pleased thee to regenerate this infant with thy Holy Spirit' – are used over every child after its baptism; and that these words settle the question beyond dispute, so far as members of the Church of England are concerned.

I desire to approach this objection with a sorrowful recollection of the sad difference of opinion which has long prevailed in my own Church upon the subject which it involves. I am quite aware of the positive assertions so frequently made, that the views of regeneration I have tried to set forth are not 'Church-views', and so forth. Such assertions go for very little with me. I have read Bishop Jewel's Apology. I do not forget what he says there about those, 'who impose upon silly men by vain and useless shows, and seek to overwhelm us with the mere name of the Church'. I am thoroughly persuaded that the views of regeneration I maintain are the views of the Prayer-Book, Articles, and Homilies of the Church of England, and I will endeavour to satisfy the reader that they are so. The more I have searched into the subject, the more thoroughly satisfied have I felt in my own mind that those who say the views I advocate are not Church views, are asserting what they cannot prove.

And now let me proceed to reply to the objection that the invariable regeneration of all infants in baptism is the doctrine of the Church of England because of the language of her baptismal service.

I answer then first of all, that the mere quotation of two isolated expressions in one particular service in our liturgy is not of itself sufficient. It must be proved that the sense in which the objector takes these expressions is the correct one. It must also be shown that this sense will bear comparison with the other services and formularies of the Church, and does not involve any contradiction. If this last point cannot be shown and proved, it is clear that the objector has put a wrong interpretation on the baptismal service, and does not understand the great principle on which all the services of our Church are drawn up.

It is a most unsound method of reasoning to take one or two expressions out of a book which has been written as one great whole, place a certain meaning upon those expressions, and then refuse to inquire whether that meaning can be reconciled with the general spirit of the rest of the book. The beginning of every heresy and erroneous tenet in religion may be traced up to this kind of reasoning, and to unfair and partial quotations.

This is precisely the Roman Catholic's argument, when he wants to prove the doctrine of transubstantiation. 'I read,' he says, 'these plain words, "This is my body, this is my blood." I want no more. I have nothing to do with your explanations and quotations from other parts of the Bible. Here is quite enough for me. The Lord Jesus Christ says, "This is my body." This settles the question.'

This again is precisely the Arian's argument, when he wants to prove that the Lord Jesus Christ is inferior to the Father. 'I read,' he says, 'these plain words, "My Father is greater than I."' It is in vain you tell him that there are other texts which show the Son to be equal with the Father, and give a different meaning to the one he has quoted. It matters not. He rests on the one single text that he has chosen to rest on, and he will hear nothing further.

This also is precisely the Socinian's argument when he wants to prove that Jesus Christ is only a man and not God. 'I read,' he tells us, 'these plain words, "The man Christ Jesus." Do not talk to me about other passages which contradict my view. All I know is here are words which cannot be mistaken, "The man Christ Jesus."'

Now without desiring to give offence, I must frankly say that I observe this kind of argument continually used in discussing the Church of England's doctrine about regeneration. People quote the words of our Baptismal Service, 'Seeing now that this child is regenerate, etc.' as an unanswerable argument in favour of all baptized infants being born again. They will frequently not listen to anything else that is brought forward from other services and formularies of the Church. They tell you they take their stand on the simple expression, 'This child is regenerate.' The words are plain, they inform us. They settle the question incontrovertibly! They seem to doubt your honesty and good sense, if you are not at once convinced. And all this time they do not see that they are taking their stand on very dangerous ground, and putting a sword into the hand of the next Socinian, Arian, or Roman Catholic, who happens to dispute with them.

I warn such people, if this tract falls into their hands, that this favourite argument will not do. A single quotation dragged out of a service will not suffice. They must prove that the meaning they attach to it is consistent with the rest of the Prayer-book, and with the Articles and Homilies. They must not expound one place of the Prayer-book, any more than of the Bible, so as to make it repugnant to another. And this, whether they mean it or not, I firmly believe they are doing.

I answer in the next place, that to say all baptized infants are regenerate, because of the expressions in the baptismal service is to contradict the great principle on which the whole Prayer-book is drawn up.

The principle of the Prayer-book is to suppose all members of the Church to be in *reality* what they are in *profession*, to be true believers in Christ, to be sanctified by the Holy Ghost. The Prayer-book takes the highest standard of what a Christian ought to be, and is all through worded accordingly. The minister addresses those who assemble together for public worship as believers. The people who use the words the liturgy puts into their mouths are supposed to be believers. But those who drew up the Prayer-book never meant for a moment to assert that all who were members of the Church of England were actually and really true Christians. On the contrary, they tell us expressly in the Articles that 'in the visible Church the evil be ever mingled with the good'. But they held that if forms of devotion were drawn up at all, they must be drawn up on the supposition that those who used them were real Christians and not false ones. And in so doing I think they were quite right. A liturgy for unbelievers and unconverted men would be absurd and practically useless. The part of the congregation for whom it was meant would care little or nothing for any liturgy at all. The holy and believing part of the congregation would find its language entirely unsuited to them.

Now this general principle of the Prayer-book is the principle on which the baptismal service is drawn up. It supposes those who bring their children to be baptized, to bring them as believers. As the seed of godly parents and children of believers, their infants are baptized. As believers, the sponsors and parents are exhorted to pray that the child may be born again, and encouraged to lay hold on the promises. And as the child of believers, the infant when baptized is pronounced regenerate, and thanks are given for it.

The principle which the Church lays down *abstractedly* is this, that baptism *when rightly and worthily received*, is a means whereby we receive inward and spiritual grace, even a death unto sin and a new birth unto righteousness.[9] But the Church cannot take upon herself to decide *particularly* when baptism is rightly and worthily received by an infant and when it is not. That an infant may receive baptism rightly the Church of England unquestionably holds, though the way and manner of it may be a hidden thing to us, for as good Archbishop Usher beautifully remarks, 'He that hath said of infants to them belongs the Kingdom of God, knows how to settle upon them the kingdom of heaven.' But to decide with positive certainty whether any one particular infant does or does not receive it rightly is beyond the Church's power. Her ministers cannot see the book of God's election. They cannot see the hidden workings of the Holy Ghost. They cannot read the hearts of parents and sponsors. They can never say of any individual child, 'this child is certainly receiving baptism unworthily.' And this being the case, the Church most wisely leans to the side of charity, assumes hopefully of each child that it receives baptism worthily, and uses language accordingly.

The men who drew up our baptismal service held that there was a connection between baptism and spiritual regeneration, and they were right.[10] They knew that there was nothing too high in the way of blessing to expect for the child of a believer. They knew that God might of His sovereign mercy give grace to any child before, or in, or at, or by the act of baptism. At all events they dared not undertake the responsibility of denying it in the case of any particular infant, and they therefore took the safer course, charitably to hope it of all. They could not draw up two services of baptism, one of a high standard of privilege, the other of a low one. They could not leave it to the option of a minister to decide when one should be used, and when the other. It would have made a minister's position at the baptismal font a most invidious one; it would have exposed him to the risk of making painful mistakes; it would have required him to decide points which none but God can decide. They prudently leaned to the side of charity. They drew up a form containing the highest standard of privilege and blessing, and wisely required that in every case of infant baptism that form and that only should be used. And in so doing they acted in the spirit of our Lord Jesus Christ's remarkable words to the seventy disciples, 'Into *whatsoever* house ye enter, first say, Peace be to this house. And if the son of peace be there, your peace shall rest upon it: if not, it shall turn to you again' (Luke 10:5, 6).

But as for maintaining as an abstract proposition that the ministerial act of baptizing a child did always necessarily convey regeneration, and that every infant baptized was invariably born again, I believe it never entered into their thoughts. In the judgment of charity and hope they supposed all to be regenerated in baptism, and used language accordingly. Whether any particular child was actually and really regenerated they left to be decided by its life and ways when it grew up. But to say that the assertions of the service are to be taken for more than a charitable supposition would throw the whole Prayer-book into confusion."

This is the only principle on which many of the *collects* can be reasonably explained. The collect for the Epiphany says, 'Grant that we who know Thee now by faith may after this life have the fruition of Thy glorious Godhead.' Will any one tell us that the compilers of the Prayer-book meant to teach, that all who use the Prayer-book do know God by faith? Surely not. The collect for Sexagesima Sunday says, 'O Lord God, who seest that we put not our trust in anything that we do, etc.' Will any dare to say that these words could ever be literally true of all members of the Church of England? Are they not manifestly a supposition? The collect for the Third Sunday after Trinity says, 'We to whom thou hast given a hearty desire to pray', etc. Who can have a doubt that this is a form of words, which is used by many of whom it could not strictly and truly be said for one minute? Who can fail to see in all these instances one uniform principle, the principle of charitably assuming that members of a Church are what they profess to be? The Church puts in the mouth of her worshipping people the sentiments and language they ought to see, and if they do not come up to her high standard the fault is theirs, not hers. But to say that by adopting such expressions she stamps and accredits all her members as real and true Christians in the sight of God would be manifestly absurd.

This is the only principle on which *the service for the churching of women* can be interpreted. Every woman for whom that service is used, is spoken of as 'the Lord's servant', and is required to answer that she 'puts her trust in the Lord'. Yet who in his senses can doubt that such words are utterly inapplicable in the case of a great proportion of those who come to be churched? They are not servants of the Lord. They do not in any sense put their trust in Him. And who would dare to argue that the compiler of the liturgy abstractedly considered that all women who were churched did really trust in the Lord, merely because they used this language? The simple explanation is, that they drew up the service on the same great principle which runs through the whole Prayer-book, the principle of charitable supposition.

This is the only principle on which *the service of baptism for people grown up* can be interpreted. In that service the minister first prays that the person about to be baptized may have the Holy Spirit given to him and be born again. The Church cannot take upon herself to pronounce decidedly that he is born again, until he has witnessed a good confession, and shown his readiness to receive the seal of baptism. Then, after that prayer, he is called upon openly to confess repentance and faith before the minister and congregation, and that being done he is baptized. Then, and not till then, comes the declaration that the person baptized is regenerate, that he is born again and made an heir of everlasting salvation. But can these words be strictly and literally true if the person baptized is a hypocrite, and has all along professed that which he does not feel? Are not the words manifestly used on the charitable supposition that he has repented and does believe, and in no other sense at all? And is it not plain to every one that in the absence of this repentance and faith, the words used are a mere form, used because the Church cannot draw up two forms, but not for a moment implying that inward and spiritual grace necessarily accompanies the outward sign, or that a death unto sin and a new birth unto righteousness is necessarily conveyed to the soul? In short the person baptized is pronounced regenerate upon the broad principle of the Prayer-book, that, in the Church services, people are charitably supposed to be what they profess to be.

This is the only intelligible principle on which *the burial service* can be interpreted. In that service the person buried is spoken of as a dear brother or sister. It is said that it hath pleased God of his great mercy to take to himself his soul. It is said, 'We give thee hearty thanks that it hath pleased thee to deliver this our brother out of the miseries of this sinful world.' It is said that our hope is this our brother rests in Christ. Now what does all this mean? Did the compilers of the Prayer-book wish us to believe that all this was strictly and literally applicable to every individual member of the Church over whose body these words were read? Will any one look the service honestly in the face and dare to say so? I cannot think it. The simple explanation of the service is, that it was drawn up, like the rest, on the presumption that all members of a Church were what they professed to be. The key to the interpretation of it is the same great principle – the principle of charitable supposition.

This is the only principle on which *the Catechism* can be interpreted. In it every child is taught to say, 'In baptism I was made a member of Christ, a child of

God, and an inheritor of the kingdom of heaven'; and a little further on, 'I learn to believe in God the Holy Ghost who sanctifieth me and all the elect people of God.' Now what does this mean? Did the Prayer-book writers intend to lay it down as an abstract principle that all baptized children are sanctified and all elect? Will any one in the present day stand forth and tell us that all the children in his parish are actually sanctified by the Holy Ghost? If he can, I can only say that his parish is an exception, or else Bible words have no meaning. But I cannot yet believe that any one would say so. I believe there is but one explanation of all these expressions in the Catechism. They are the words of charitable supposition, and in no other sense can they be taken.[12]

I lay these things before any one who fancies that all children are regenerated in baptism, because of the expression in the Prayer-book service, and I ask him to weigh them well. I am not to be moved from my ground by hard names, and bitter epithets, and insinuations that I am not a real Churchman. I am not to be shaken by scraps and sentences torn from their places, and thrust isolated and alone upon our notice. What I say is, that in interpreting the baptismal service of the Church we must be consistent.

Men say that the view of the service I maintain is 'non-natural and dishonest'. I deny the charge altogether. I might retort it on many of those who make it. Whose view is most unnatural, I ask the Reader? Is it the view of the man who expounds the baptismal service on one principle, and the burial service on another – or is it my view, which interprets all on one uniform and the same system?

We must be consistent, I repeat. I refuse to interpret one part of the Prayer-book on one principle, and another part on another. The expressions to which I have been calling the Reader's attention are either abstract dogmatic declarations, or charitable assumptions and suppositions. They cannot be both. And I now call upon those who hold all children to be invariably regenerated, because of strong expressions in the baptismal service, to carry out their principles honestly, fairly, fully, and consistently, if they can.

If all children are actually regenerated in baptism, because the service says, 'This child is regenerate', then by parity of reasoning it follows that all people who use the collect have faith, and a hearty desire to pray, all women who are churched put their trust in the Lord, all members of the Church who are buried are dear brethren, and we hope rest in Christ, and all children who say the Catechism are sanctified by the Holy Ghost, and are elect. Consistency demands it. Fair interpretation of words demands it. There is not a jot of evidence to show that those are not really sanctified and elect who say the Catechism, if you once maintain that those are all actually regenerated over whom the words of the baptismal service have been used.

But if I am to be told that the children who use the Catechism are not necessarily all elect and sanctified, and that the people buried are not necessarily all resting in Christ, and that the language in both cases is that of charitable supposition, then I reply, in common fairness let us be allowed to take the language of the baptismal service in the same sense. I see one uniform principle running through all the Prayer-book, through all the offices, through all the devotional formularies of the Church. That principle is the principle of charitable supposition. Following that principle, I can make good sense, and good divinity of every service in the book. Without that principle I cannot. On that principle therefore I take my stand. If I say all baptized children are regenerate, because of certain words in the baptismal service, I contradict that principle. I believe our services were meant to be consistent one with another, and not contradictory. I therefore cannot say so.

My next answer to those who say all baptized persons are regenerate, because of the baptismal service, is this – that such a view would not agree with the Thirty-nine Articles.

Now I am aware that many have a very low opinion of the Articles. Many seem to know little about them, and to attach little weight to any quotation from them. 'The Prayer-book, the Prayer-book!' is the watchword of these people; all we have to do with is, what does the Prayer-book say? I disagree with such persons entirely. I look upon the Thirty-nine Articles as the Church of England's confession of faith. I believe the words of the declaration which prefaces them, are strictly true, 'That the Articles of the Church of England do contain the true doctrine of the Church of England,' and that any doctrine which does not entirely harmonise with those Articles is not the doctrine of the Church. I honour and love the book of Common Prayer, but I do not call it the Church's confession of faith. I delight in it as an incomparable manual of public worship, but if I want to ascertain the deliberate judgment of the Church upon any point of doctrine, I turn first to the Articles. What would a Lutheran or Scotch Presbyterian say of me, if I judged his Church by his minister's prayers, and did not judge by the Augsburg or Westminster Confessions? I do not say this in order to disparage the Prayer-book, but to point out calmly what it really is. I want to place the Thirty-nine Articles in their proper position before the Reader's mind, and so to make him see the real value of what they say. It is a circumstance deeply to be regretted that the Articles are not more read and studied by members of the Church of England.

I will now ask the reader to observe the striking prominence which the Articles everywhere give to the Bible as the only rule of faith. The sixth article says that 'Whatsoever is not read in Holy Scripture, nor may be proved thereby is not to be required of any man that it should be believed as an article of the faith, or be thought requisite or necessary to salvation.' The eighth says, that the 'three creeds ought thoroughly to be received and believed, for they may be proved by most certain warrant of Holy Scripture.' The twentieth says, that 'It is not lawful for the Church to ordain anything that is contrary to God's word written, neither may it so expound one place of Scripture that it be repugnant to another.' The twenty-first says, that 'things ordained by General Councils as necessary to salvation have neither strength nor authority, unless it may be declared that they be taken out of Holy Scripture.' The twenty-second condemns certain Romish doctrines, because they 'are grounded upon no warranty of Scripture, but are rather repugnant to the word of God.' The twenty-eighth condemns transubstantiation, because it 'cannot be proved by Holy Writ, but is repugnant to the plain words of Scripture.' The thirty-fourth says that traditions and ceremonies of the Church may be changed, so long as 'nothing be ordained against God's word.'

Now I think that all these quotations make it perfectly certain that the Bible is the sole rule of faith in the Church of England, and that nothing is a doctrine of the Church which cannot be entirely reconciled with the word of God. And I see here a complete answer to those who say we make an idol of the Bible, and tell us we ought to go first to the Prayer-book, or to the opinion of the primitive Church. I see also that the meaning placed upon any part of the Prayer-

book which at all disagrees with the Bible, and cannot
be proved by the Bible, must be an incorrect meaning.
I am not to listen to any interpretation of any service in
the liturgy, which cannot be thoroughly reconciled with
Scripture. It may sound very plausible. It may be
defended very speciously. But does it in any way
jar with plain texts in the Bible? If it does, there is
a mistake somewhere. There is a flaw in the
interpretation. On the very face of it, it is incorrect.
It is utterly absurd to suppose that the founders of
our Church would assert the supremacy of
Scripture seven or eight times over, and then draw
up a service in the Prayer-book at all inconsistent
with Scripture. And unless the doctrine that all
children baptized are necessarily regenerated in
baptism can first be shown to be in the Bible, it is a
mere waste of time to begin any discussion of the
subject by talking of the Prayer-book.

I ask the reader in the next place to observe what
the twenty-fifth and twenty-sixth articles say. The
twenty-fifth speaks generally of sacraments; and it
says of them – both of baptism and of the Lord's
supper – 'In such only as worthily receive the same
they have a wholesome effect or operation.' The
twenty-sixth speaks of the unworthiness of
ministers not hindering the effects of the sacraments.
It says, 'Neither is the effect of Christ's ordinance
taken away by their wickedness, nor the grace of God's
gifts diminished from such as by faith and rightly do

receive the sacraments.' Here we have a broad general principle twice asserted. The benefit of either sacrament is clearly confined to such as *rightly, worthily, and with faith* receive it. The Romish notion of all alike getting good from it, 'ex opere operato', is as clearly pointed at and rejected. Now can this be reconciled with the doctrine that all who are baptized are at once invariably regenerated? I say decidedly that it cannot.

I ask the reader in the next place to observe the language of the article about baptism, the twenty-seventh. It says, 'Baptism is not only a sign of profession and mark of difference, whereby Christian men are discerned from others that are not christened, but it is also a sign of regeneration or new birth, whereby, as by an instrument, they that receive baptism rightly are grafted into the Church; the promises of forgiveness of sin and of our adoption to be the sons of God by the Holy Ghost are visibly signed and sealed; faith is confirmed and grace increased by virtue of prayer unto God. The baptism of young children is in any wise to be retained in the Church as most agreeable with the institution of Christ.' Nothing can be more striking than the wise caution of all this language when contrasted with the statements about baptism with which our ears are continually assailed in this day. There is not a word said which might lead us to suppose that a different principle is to be applied to the baptism of infants, from that which has been already laid down about all sacraments in the twenty-fifth article. We are left to the inevitable conclusion that in all cases *worthy reception* is essential to the full efficacy of the sacrament. There is not a word said about a great inward and spiritual blessing invariably and necessarily attending the baptism of an infant. There is a perfect silence on that head, and a most speaking silence too. Surely a doctrine involving such immense and important consequences as the universal spiritual regeneration of all infants in baptism would never have been passed over in entire silence, if it had been the doctrine of the Church. The authors of the articles unquestionably knew the importance of the document they were drawing up. Unquestionably they weighed well every word and every statement they put down on paper. And yet they are perfectly silent on the subject. That silence is like the silence of Scripture, a great fact, and one which can never be got over.

I ask the reader in the next place to observe what the thirteenth article says. It tells us that 'Works done before the grace of Christ and the inspiration of His Spirit are not pleasant to God', etc. Here we are plainly taught that works may be done by men before grace and the Spirit are given to them, and this too by baptized members of the Church, for it is for them that the articles are drawn up. But how can this be reconciled with the notion that all baptized persons are necessarily regenerated? How can any person be regenerated without having the grace of Christ and the inspiration of the Spirit? There is only one view on which the article can be reasonably explained. That view is the simple one, that many baptized people are not regenerate, have no grace and no indwelling of the Spirit, and that it is their case before they are born again and converted, which is here described.

The last article I will ask the reader to observe is the seventeenth. The subject of that article is predestination and election. It is a subject which many people dislike exceedingly, and are ready to stop their ears whenever it is mentioned. I acknowledge freely that it is a deep subject. But there stands the article. It cannot be denied that it forms part of our Church's confession of faith. Whether men like it or not, they must not talk as if it did not exist, in discussing the subject of the Church's doctrines. The article begins with laying down the great truth that God 'hath constantly decreed by his counsel secret to us, to deliver from curse and damnation those whom he hath chosen in Christ out of mankind and to bring them by Christ to everlasting salvation.' It then proceeds to describe the calling of these persons by God's Spirit, and the consequences of that calling; 'they through grace obey the calling: they be justified freely: *they be made sons of God by adoption*: they be made like the image of his only begotten son Jesus Christ; they walk religiously in good works, and at length by God's mercy they attain to everlasting felicity.' Now all I ask the reader to consider is this, did the writers of the articles mean to say that these persons were a separate and distinct class from those who were regenerated or not? We must think so if we consider baptism is always accompanied by regeneration. The things spoken of in this description are things of which multitudes of baptized persons know nothing at all. I do not however believe that such an idea ever entered into the minds of those who wrote the articles. I believe that they looked on election, justification, adoption and regeneration, as the peculiar privileges of a certain number, but not of all members of the visible Church, and that just as all baptized people are not elect, justified and sanctified, so also all baptized people are not regenerated. Very striking is the difference between the language of the article which treats of baptism, and the article which treats of election. In the former we find the cautious general statement, that in baptism 'the promises of our adoption to be the sons of God *are visibly signed and sealed*'. In the latter we find the broad assertion that the elect '*be made the sons of God* by adoption'.

Such is the doctrine of the articles. If regeneration be what the Catechism describes it, 'a death unto sin and a new birth unto righteousness', I cannot find the slightest ground in the articles for the notion that all baptized persons are necessarily regenerate. There is an absence of any direct assertion of such a doctrine. There are several passages which appear completely inconsistent with it. I cannot suppose that the articles and liturgy were meant to be contrary one to the other. The men who drew up the Thirty-nine Articles in 1562 were the men who compiled the Prayer-book in 1549. They drew up the articles with a certain and distinct knowledge of the contents of the Prayer-book. Yet the interpretation of the baptismal service I am contending against would make the one formulary contradictory to the other. The conclusion I come to is clear and decided – such an interpretation cannot be correct.

My last answer to those who say that all baptized persons are necessarily regenerated, because of the wording of the baptismal service, is this: such a doctrine would make the Prayer-book disagree with the Homilies of the Church of England.

The Homilies are not liked by some persons any more than the thirty-nine articles. No doubt they are human compositions and therefore not perfect. No doubt they contain words and expressions here and there which might be amended. But after all the members of the Church of England are bound to recollect that the thirty-fifth article expressly asserts that they contain 'a godly and wholesome doctrine'. Whatever their deficiencies may be, the general tone of their doctrine is clear and unmistakeable. And any interpretation of the Prayer-book services, which makes those services inconsistent with the Homilies, must, on the very face of it, be an incorrect interpretation.

Let me then call the reader's attention to the following passages in the Homilies:

In the Homily of Charity there are the following passages. 'What thing can we wish so good for us, as the heavenly Father to reckon and take us for *his children*? And this shall we be sure of, saith Christ, if we love every man without exception. And if we do otherwise, saith he, we be no better than the Pharisees, Publicans and Heathens, and shall have our reward with them, that is to be shut out from the number of God's chosen children, and from his everlasting inheritance in heaven.' Again, 'Thus have I set forth unto you what charity is as well by the doctrine as by the example of Christ himself: whereby also every man may without error know himself, what state and condition he standeth in, whether he be in charity, and so *the child of the Father* in heaven or not.' And again, 'He that beareth a good heart and mind, and useth well his tongue and deeds unto every man, friend or foe, he may know thereby that he hath charity. And then he is sure also that Almighty God taketh him for *his dearly beloved son*; as Saint John saith, hereby manifestly are known the children of God from the children of the devil; for whosoever doth not love his brother belongeth not unto God.'

In the Homily of Almsdeeds there is this passage, 'God of his mercy and special favour towards them whom he hath appointed to everlasting salvation, hath so offered his grace especially, and they have so received it faithfully, that, although by reason of their sinful living outwardly they seemed before to have been the children of wrath and perdition, yet, now, the Spirit of God working mightily in them, unto obedience to

God's will and commandments, they declare by their outward deeds and life, in the shewing of mercy and charity – which cannot come but of the Spirit of God and his especial grace – that they are *the undoubted children of God* appointed to everlasting life. And so, by their wickedness and ungodly living they showed themselves, according to the judgment of men which follow the outward appearance, to be reprobates and castaways, so now by their obedience unto God's holy will, and by their mercifulness and tender pity – wherein they show themselves to be like unto God who is the fountain and spring of all mercy – they declare openly and manifestly unto the sight of men that they are *the sons of God*, and elect of him into salvation.'

In the Homily for Whitsunday I read the following passages, 'If any man be a dumb Christian, not professing his faith openly, but cloaking and colouring himself for fear of danger in time to come, he giveth men occasion, justly and with good conscience, to doubt lest he *have not the grace of the Holy Ghost* within him, because he is tongue-tied and cannot speak.' Again, 'It is the Holy Ghost and no other thing, that doth quicken the minds of men, stirring up good and godly motions in their hearts, which are agreeable to the will and commandment of God, such as otherwise of their own crooked and perverse nature they should never have. That which is born of the flesh, saith Christ, is flesh, and that which is born of the spirit is spirit. As who should say, man of his own nature is fleshy and carnal, corrupt and naught, sinful and disobedient to God, without any spark of goodness in him, without any virtuous or godly notion, only given to evil thoughts and wicked deeds. As for the works of the Spirit, the fruits of faith, charitable and godly motions – if he have any at all in him – they proceed only of the Holy Ghost who is the only worker of our sanctification, and maketh us new men in Christ Jesus. Did not God's Holy Spirit work in the child David, when from a poor shepherd he became a princely prophet? Did not God's Holy Spirit miraculously work in Matthew, sitting at the receipt of custom, when of a proud publican he became a humble and lowly evangelist? And who can choose but marvel to consider that Peter should become, of a simple fisher, a chief and mighty apostle? Paul of a cruel and bloody persecutor, to teach the Gentiles? Such is the power of the Holy Ghost to regenerate men, and as it were to bring them forth anew, so that they shall be nothing like the men that they were before. Neither doth he think it sufficient inwardly to work the spiritual and new birth of man, unless he do also dwell and abide in him. O what comfort is this to the heart of a true Christian to think that the Holy Ghost dwelleth within him!'

And then comes the following passage which I request the reader specially to observe. 'How shall I know that the Holy Ghost is within me? some men perchance will say. Forsooth as the tree is known by his fruit, so is also the Holy Ghost. The fruits of the Holy Ghost, according to the mind of St. Paul, are these: love, joy, peace, long-suffering, etc. Contrariwise the deeds of the flesh are these: adultery, fornication, uncleanness, wantonness, idolatry, witchcraft, hatred, debate, emulation, wrath, contention, sedition, heresy, envy, murder, drunkenness, gluttony, and such like. Here is now that glass, where thou must behold thyself, and discern whether thou have the Holy Ghost within thee or the spirit of the flesh. If thou see that thy works are virtuous and good, consonant to the prescribed rule of God's word, savouring and tasting not of the flesh but of the spirit; then assure thyself that thou art endued with the Holy Ghost: otherwise in thinking well of thyself thou dost nothing but deceive thyself.' Once more, 'To conclude and make an end ye shall briefly take this short lesson; wheresoever ye find the spirit of arrogance and pride, the spirit of envy, hatred, contention, cruelty, murder, extortion, witchcraft, necromancy, etc., assure yourselves that there is the spirit of the devil and not of God, albeit they pretend outwardly to the world never so much holiness. For as the gospel teacheth us, the spirit of Jesus is a good spirit, an holy spirit, a sweet spirit, a lowly spirit, a merciful spirit, full of charity and love, full of forgiveness and pity, not rendering evil for evil, extremity for extremity, but overcoming evil with good, and remitting all offence even from the heart. According to which rule, if any man live uprightly, of him it may safely be pronounced that he hath the Holy Ghost within him: if not, then it is a plain token that he doth usurp the name of the Holy Ghost in vain.'

I lay these passages before the reader in their naked simplicity. I will not weary him with long comments upon them. In fact none are needed. Two things, I think, are abundantly evident. One is, that in the judgment of the Homilies no men are the undoubted children of God and sons of God, and elect unto salvation, unless it is proved by their charity and good works. The other is, that no man has the Holy Ghost within him, in the judgment of the Homilies, except he brings forth the fruits of the Spirit in his life. But all this is flatly contradictory to the doctrine of those who say that all baptized persons are necessarily regenerate. They tell us that all people are made the children of God by virtue of their baptism – whatever be their manner of living – and must be addressed as such all their lives; and that all people have the grace of the Holy Ghost within them, by virtue of their baptism, and must be considered regenerate whatever fruits they may be bringing forth in their daily habits and conversation. According to this, the Homilies say one thing, and the Prayer-book says another. I leave the reader to judge whether it is in the least degree probable that this can be the case. These Homilies were put forth by authority in the year 1562, and appointed to be read in Churches, in order to supply the deficiency of good preaching, and when they had been once read they were to be 'repeated and read again'. And yet according to the interpretation of the baptismal service I am contending against, these Homilies contradict the Prayer-book! Surely it is difficult to avoid the conclusion which I most unhesitatingly come to myself, that a system of interpreting the baptismal service which sets the Prayer-book at variance with the Homilies, as well as with the articles, must be incorrect.

I leave the subject of the Church of England's views about regeneration here. I wish I could have spoken of it more shortly. But I have been anxious to meet the objections drawn from the baptismal service fully, openly, and face to face. I have no doubt in my own mind as to the true doctrine of the Church in the question. But many, I know, have been troubled and perplexed about it, and few appear to me to see the matter as clearly as they might. And it is to supply such persons with information, as well as to meet the arguments of adversaries, that I have gone into the question so fully as I have.

Other points might easily be dealt upon, which would serve to throw even more light on the subject, and see, still further to bear out the views that I maintain, as to the real doctrine of the Church of England about regeneration.

Is it not notorious, for instance, that the Article about Baptism in our confession of faith was entirely altered, and brought into its present form, when Edward the Sixth came to the throne? Our Reformers found an Article drawn up in 1536, in which the doctrine of grace always accompanying the Baptism of Infants was plainly and unmistakably asserted. The Articles of 1536 say, 'By the Sacrament of Baptism, infants, innocents, and children, do also obtain remission of their sins, the grace and favour of God, and be made thereby the very sons and children of God.' The Reformers of our Church in drawing up the Articles of 1552, entirely abstained from making any such assertion. They framed our present Article on Baptism, in which no such unqualified statement can be found. Now, why did they do so? Why did they not adopt the language of the old Article, if they really believed its doctrine? Let any one answer these questions. Did it not plainly mean that they did not approve of the doctrine of the invariable regeneration of Infants in Baptism?

Again, is it not notorious that the Irish Articles of 1615 have never been replaced or disannulled by the Church of Ireland? Subscription to the Articles is undoubtedly not required at Irish ordinations. Subscription to the Thirty-nine Articles only is held sufficient. But it was distinctly understood, when the Thirty-nine Articles were received by the Irish Church, in 1634, that their reception did not imply any slur on the Irish Articles, and only testified the agreement of the Church of Ireland with that of England, both in doctrine and discipline. Now these Irish Articles most plainly declare that the regenerate are the elect, the justified, the believers, the true Christians, who persevere unto the end; and no less plainly imply, that those who are not true believers are not regenerate. There can be no mistake about this. No man, I think, can read these Articles and not see it. And yet there is the closest union between the Church of England and the Church of Ireland, and always has been.

How could this be, if the Church of Ireland's view about the regenerate had always been considered false and heretical? Why were the Irish Articles not rejected as unsound, when for uniformity's sake, the English Articles were received? How was it, that for many years after 1634, the Irish Bishops always required subscription to both Irish and English Articles at their ordinations? Let these questions also be answered. Did it not show plainly that the two Churches were not thought to be at variance upon the subject of regeneration?[13]

Again, is it not notorious that almost all the Bishops and leading divines who took part in the Reformation of our Church, were men who held opinions which, right or wrong, are called Calvinistic, and in the main were thoroughly agreed with those clergy who are termed Evangelical in the present day? There is no room for doubt on this point. It has been allowed by many who do not approve of Evangelical opinions themselves. They were in frequent communication with the leading Swiss Reformers. They procured the help of men like Peter Martyr and Bucer, to assist them in carrying on the work of Reformation. And yet men want us to believe that our Reformers deliberately framed a baptismal service containing a doctrine which is inconsistent with their own views. Is it likely, is it reasonable, is it agreeable to common sense, to suppose they would do such a thing? And is it not an acknowledged axiom in interpreting all public documents, such as oaths, articles of faith, and religious formularies, that they are always to be interpreted in the sense of those who drew them up and imposed them?[14]

There is a passage in Bishop Sanderson's Prelections on the Obligation of an Oath, to the same effect.

But I leave all these points, and hasten on to a conclusion. I have tried to show the reader the *nature*, *necessity* and *marks* of regeneration. I have also endeavoured to *answer the objections* most commonly advanced against the views that I hold. I deeply feel that I have not done justice to my cause; but I trust at any rate I have said enough to show that the argument is not so entirely on one side as some men affirm, and to supply every reader with matter for private thought. It only remains for me now to wind up all I have said with a few words of solemn appeal to every one into whose hands this tract may happen to fall.

I say 'solemn appeal', and I say it advisedly. I feel strongly the immense importance of sound and Scriptural views of the whole question I have been considering. I feel it especially as respects that part of it which touches the doctrine of the Church of England. Men sometimes say it makes no difference whether we think all baptized persons are regenerate or not. They tell us it all comes to the same thing in the long run. I cannot say so. To my humble apprehension it seems to make an immense difference. If I tell a man that he has grace in his heart, and only needs to stir up a gift already within him, it is one thing. If I tell him that he is dead in sins, and must be born again, it is quite another. The moral effect of the two messages must, on the very face of it, be widely different. The one, I contend, is calculated by God's blessing to awaken the sinner. The other, I contend, is calculated to lull him to sleep. The one, I maintain, is likely to feed sloth, check self-examination, and encourage an easy self-satisfied state of soul; he has got some grace within him whenever he likes to use it, why should he be in a hurry, why be afraid? The other, I maintain, is likely to rouse convictions, drive him to self-inquiry, and frighten him out of his dangerous security, he has nothing within him to rest upon, he must find a refuge and remedy, he is lost and perishing, what must he do to be saved? The one message, I affirm, is likely to keep men natural men, the other to make them spiritual men; the one to have no effect upon the conscience, the other to lead to Christ. Let men say what they will, I, for one, dare not say I think it all comes to the same thing.

I see fresh reason continually for dreading the doctrine that all baptized persons are regenerate. I hear of laymen who once did run well, losing their first love, and appearing to make shipwreck of their faith. I hear of ministers, who once bade fair to be pillars in the Church, stumbling at this stumbling-stone, and marring all their usefulness. I see the doctrine leavening and spoiling the religion of many private Christians, and insensibly paving the way for a long train of unscriptural notions. I see it interfering with every leading doctrine of the gospel; it encourages men to believe that election, adoption, justification and the indwelling of the Spirit are all conferred on them in baptism; and then, to avoid the difficulties which such a system entails, the fulness of all these mighty truths is pared down, mutilated and explained away; or else the minds of congregations are bewildered with contradictory and inconsistent statements. I see it ultimately producing in some minds a mere sacramental Christianity; a Christianity in which there is much said about union with Christ, but it is a union begun only by baptism, and kept up only by the Lord's Supper; a Christianity in which the leading doctrines that the Apostle Paul dwells on in almost all his epistles, have nothing but a subordinate position; a Christianity in which Christ has not His rightful office, and faith has not its rightful place. I see all this, and mourn over it unfeignedly. I cannot think that the subject I am urging on the reader's attention is one of secondary importance. And once more I say, I cannot leave him without a solemn appeal to his conscience, whoever he may be, into whose hands this tract may fall.

I appeal to all men who love the Bible, and make it their standard of truth and error; and in saying this, I address myself especially to all members of the Church of England. I ask you to observe the manner of living of multitudes of baptized persons on every side of you. I ask you to observe how their hearts are entirely set on this world, and buried in its concerns. And I then ask you, are they born of God? If you say, Yes! I answer, how can that he, when your

Bible expressly says, 'He that is born of God doeth righteousness, and doth not commit sin?' (1 John 2:29; 3:9). Are they children of God? If you say, Yes! I answer, How can that be, when the Bible says expressly, 'In this the children of God are manifest and the children of the devil; whosoever doeth not righteousness is not of God' (1 John 3:10). Are they sons of God? If you say, Yes! I answer, How can that be, when the Bible says expressly, 'As many as are led by the Spirit of God, they are the sons of God' (Rom. 8:14). What will you say to these things? Surely you will not turn your back upon the Bible.

I appeal next to all who love the good old rule of the Bible, 'every tree is known by his own fruit' (Luke 6:44). I ask you to try the great bulk of professing Christians by the fruits they bring forth, and to say what kind of fruits they are. Is it not perfectly true that many baptized persons know little or nothing of the fruits of the Spirit, and much, only too much, of the works of the flesh? Is it not certain that they are destitute of those marks of being born of God which the Bible describes? What will you say to these things? Surely if you abide by your old principle you will hardly say that all baptized people have within them the Holy Spirit.

I appeal next to all who love the Church Catechism, and profess to be guided by its statements about the sacraments. You are aware that the inward and spiritual grace of baptism is there said to be 'a death unto sin and a new birth unto righteousness'. I ask you, as in the sight of God, to say whether any evidence whatever of this grace can be seen in the lives of many baptized persons. Where is their deadness to sin? They live in it. It is their element. Where is their new birth unto righteousness? They are habitual 'servants of sin, and free from righteousness' (Rom. 6:20). Sin reigns and rules in their mortal bodies. They are enemies of all righteousness. What will you say to these things? Surely you will not tell us, that the outward and visible sign is always attended by the inward and spiritual grace. If so, grace and no grace are the same thing.

I appeal, lastly, to all who dread antinomianism and licentious doctrine. You have heard of those wretched persons who profess to glory in Christ and free grace, and yet think it no shame to live immoral lives, and continue in wilful sin. You think such conduct horrible, an insult to the Lord Jesus, and a disgrace to Christianity. And you are right to think so. But what will you say to the doctrine that a man may have the Holy Spirit, and yet not bring forth the fruits of the Spirit, may have grace in his heart, and yet show no sign of it in his life? What will you say to these things? Surely, if you are consistent you will recoil from the idea of dishonouring the third Person of the blessed Trinity, no less than you do from dishonouring the Lord Himself. Surely you will shrink from saying that all baptized persons have the Holy Ghost.

And now, reader, I leave this subject in your hands, and I heartily pray God to guide you by His

Spirit to a right understanding of it. I ask you to compare what I have said with the Bible, and I invite you to give the whole question your calm consideration and your earnest prayers. If in the course of this tract I have said anything that hurts your feelings, I am sorry for it and ask pardon. If I have said anything contrary to the truth as it is in Jesus, I hope the Lord will make me see it. But I think I can say with a good conscience, that I have stated nothing about regeneration which I do not honestly believe to be the doctrine of the Bible, and the doctrine of the Church of England.

Once for all I protest against the charge that I am no true Churchman because I hold the opinions that I do. In the matter of true and real attachment of the Church of England, I will not give place by subjection to those who are called High Churchmen for one moment. Have they signed the Thirty-nine Articles *ex animo* and *bona fide*? So have I. Have they declared their full assent to the liturgy and all things contained in it? So have I. Do they think Episcopacy the best form of Church government? So do I. Do they honour the Sacraments? So do I. Do they think them generally necessary to salvation? So do I. Do they labour for the prosperity of the Church? So do I. Do they urge on their congregation the privileges of the Church of England? So do I. Do they deprecate all needless secession and separation from her ranks? So do I. Do they oppose the enemies of the Church, both Romish and Infidel? So do I. Do they love the Prayer-book of the Church of England? So do I. I repudiate with indignation the unworthy imputation that I interpret any part of that Prayer-book in a dishonest or unnatural sense. I am content with the Prayer-book as it is. I ask for no alteration. I dread attempts to alter and unsettle what is already good. I have read too much already of men who in trying to mend one fancied defect make two more. My desire is that the Prayer-book may be let alone.

But one thing I cannot see to be essential, in order to prove myself a true Churchman. I cannot see that I ought to hold doctrines which made the Prayer-book clash and jar with the Articles and Homilies. I cannot see that I must hold that all baptized persons are necessarily and invariably born again. I protest against the system of making the baptismal register the great evidence of our regeneration, and not our lives. I recoil from the idea that a man may have grace, and yet nobody see it in his behaviour; may have a new heart and yet none discover it in his conduct; may have the Holy Spirit and yet no fruit of the Spirit appear in any of his ways. I consider that such a notion affects the honour of the Holy Ghost and the cause of true holiness, and I dare not allow it. I consider it throws confusion over the whole system of Christ's Gospel, and involves the necessity of calling things in religion by wrong names, and I dare not allow it. I think as highly of baptism as any one, when rightly received. I count churchmanship a privilege. But I think regeneration a higher privilege still, and one to which, unhappily, many baptized Churchmen never attain.

I deny that I hold any new doctrine about regeneration, in saying this. I appeal to the Bible. I appeal to the Articles. I appeal to the Prayer-book. I appeal to the Homilies. In all of them I say unhesitatingly I see the doctrine I maintain. I appeal to the writings of all the principal Reformers of our Church. I appeal to the works of some of the best and worthiest Bishops who have ever adorned the Bench. I assert confidently that it has been preached in Church of England pulpits ever since the time of the Reformation: in many at some periods, in some at all. There never has been wanting a succession of faithful men, who have constantly said to the mass of their congregation, 'Ye must be born again'. There never was an attempt to shut the door against a minister for preaching such doctrine before our own day. In short if I err, I feel that I err in good company. I err with Bishop Hooper and Bishop Latimer, those faithful martyrs of Christ. I err with Jewel, and Leighton, and Usher, and Hall, and Hopkins, and Carleton, and Davenant, and many others of whom I have not time to speak particularly. And when I think of this, I am not disturbed by the charge that I do not agree with Archbishop Laud and the Non-jurors, or even with others of later date still.

Reader, I commend you to God, and to the word of His grace. You and I are travelling to a place where controversies will all be forgotten, and nothing but eternal realities remain. Would you have a real hope in that day? See to it that you have a real regeneration. Nothing else will do. 'Except a man be born again, he cannot see the kingdom of God' (John 3:3).

REFERENCES

Chapter 1

1. 'There be two manner of men. Some there be that be not justified, nor regenerated, nor yet in the state of salvation; that is to say, not God's servants. They lack the renovation or regeneration; they be not come yet to Christ' (*Bishop Latimer's Sermons*, 1552).

2. The reader must not suppose there is anything new or modern in this statement. It would be an endless work to quote passages from standard divines of the Church of England, in which the words, 'regenerate and unregenerate' are used to describe the difference which I have been speaking of. The pious and godly members of the Church are called 'the regenerate' – the worldly and ungodly are called 'the unregenerate'. I think no one well read in English divinity, can question this for a moment.

3. 'All these expressions set forth the same work of grace upon the heart, though they may be understood under different notions' (*Bishop Hopkins*, 1670).

4. 'The preaching of the word is the great means which God hath appointed for regeneration: "faith cometh by hearing, and hearing by the word of God" (Rom. 10:17). When God first created man, it is said that "he breathed into his nostrils the breath of life", but when God new creates man, he breathes into his ears. This is that word that raised the dead, calling them out of the grave: this is that word that opens the eyes of the blind, that turns the hearts of the disobedient and rebellious. And though wicked and profane men scoff at preaching, and count all ministers' words and God's words too, but so much wind, yet they are such wind, believe it, as is able to tear rocks and rend mountains; such wind as, if ever they are saved, must shake and overturn the foundations of all their carnal confidence and presumption. Be exhorted therefore more to prize and more to frequent the preaching of the word' (*Bishop Hopkins*, 1670).

5. 'The Scripture carries it, that no more than a child can beget itself, or a dead man quicken himself, or a nonentity create itself; no more can any carnal man regenerate himself, or work true saving grace in his own soul' (*Bishop Hopkins*, 1670).

'There are two kinds of baptism, and both necessary: the one interior, which is the cleansing of the heart, the drawing of the

Father, the operation of the Holy Ghost: and this baptism is in man when he believeth and trusteth that Christ is the only method of his salvation' (*Bishop Hooper*, 1547).

'It is on all parts gladly confessed, that there may be, in divers cases, life by virtue of inward baptism, where outward is not found' (*Richard Hooker*, 1592).

'There is a baptism of the Spirit as of water' (*Bishop Jeremy Taylor*, 1660).

6. 'The mixture of those things by speech, which by nature are divided, is the mother of all error' (*Hooker*, 1595).

7. For instance, Bishop Davenant and Bishop Hopkins frequently speak of a 'sacramental regeneration', when they are handling the subject of baptism, as a thing entirely distinct from spiritual regeneration. The general tenor of their writings is to speak of the godly as the regenerate, and the ungodly as the unregenerate. But with every feeling of respect for two such good men, the question yet remains – what Scripture warrant have we for saying there are two regenerations? I answer unhesitatingly, we have none at all.

Chapter 2

1. 'Tell me, thou that in holy duties grudgest at every word that is spoken; that thinkest every summons to the public worship as unpleasant as the sound of thy passing bell; that sayest, "When will the Sabbath be gone, and the ordinances be over?" What wilt thou do in heaven? What shall such an unholy heart do there, where a Sabbath shall be as long as eternity itself; where there shall be nothing but holy duties; and where there shall not be a spare minute, so much as for a vain thought, or an idle word? What wilt thou do in heaven, where whatsoever thou shalt hear, see or converse with, all is holy? And by how much more perfect the holiness of heaven is than that of the saints on earth, by so much the more irksome and intolerable would it be to wicked men, for if they cannot endure the weak light of a star, how will they be able to endure the dazzling light of the sun itself?' (*Bishop Hopkins*, 1670).

2. 'Make sure to yourselves this great change. It is no notion that I have now preached unto you. Your natures and your lives

must be changed, or, believe it, you will be found at the last day under the wrath of God. For God will not change or alter the word that is gone out of his mouth; he hath said it; Christ, who is the truth and word of God, hath pronounced it, that without the new birth, or regeneration, no man shall inherit the kingdom of God' (*Bishop Hopkins*, 1670).

3. 'Regeneration, or the new birth, is of absolute necessity unto eternal life. There is no other change simply necessary, but only this. If thou art poor, thou mayest so continue, and yet be saved. If thou art despised, thou mayest so continue, and yet be saved. If thou art unlearned, thou mayest so continue, and yet be saved. Only one change is necessary. If thou art wicked and ungodly, and continuest so, Christ, who hath the keys of heaven, who shutteth and no man openeth, hath Himself doomed thee, that thou shalt in no wise enter into the kingdom of God' (*Bishop Hopkins*, 1670).

Chapter 3

1. 'The interpretation of this place that I judge to be the most natural and unforced is this: "He that is born of God doth not commit sin"; that is, he doth not sin in that malignant manner in which the children of the devil do: he doth not make a trade of sin, nor live in the constant and allowed practice of it. There is a great difference betwixt regenerate and unregenerate persons in the very sins that they commit. All indeed sin; but a child of God cannot sin, that is, though he doth sin, yet he cannot sin after such a manner as wicked and unregenerate men do' (*Bishop Hopkins*, 1670).

2. 'Let none conclude that they have no grace, because they have many imperfections in their obedience. Thy grace may be very weak and imperfect, and yet thou mayest be truly born again to God, and be a genuine son and heir of heaven' (*Bishop Hopkins*, 1670).

3. 'Love to those who are truly godly, is a certain and infallible sign of regeneration. This is a certain sign that a mighty change is wrought on the heart; for naturally we are inclined to hate the children

of God, upon that very account because they are godly.' 'It is in vain to think that we are born of God, if we have not a sincere and cordial affection for all those that are the children of God and our brethren' (*Bishop Hopkins*, 1670).

4. The reader who would like to know the opinion of Augustine on this argument from the First Epistle of John is referred to the following extract from his writings. How it is that men can assert that the views of regeneration I maintain are new and modern views, in the face of such a passage, from such a father as Augustine, I leave to others to explain.

'Behold a man when baptized has received the sacrament of his nativity. He hath a sacrament, and a great sacrament; divine, holy, ineffable. Consider what it is; that it should even make a new man, by the remission of all sins. Let him however attend to his heart: whether that be there perfected, which has been done in his body. Let him see whether he has charity; and then let him say, I have been born of God. If he hath it not, he hath indeed a character impressed upon him: but he only wanders about as a deserter. Let him have charity: otherwise let him not say, that he has been born of God.

But I have, says he, the sacrament. Here then the Apostle: If I know all sacraments, and have all faith, so that I could remove mountains, yet have not charity, I am nothing.

In the whole of St. John's Epistle, nothing is so much commended as charity: insomuch that if he seem to introduce other subjects, he constantly returns to that topic, and would always refer to charity, whatsoever he may happen to introduce.

Let me see then whether he does not do it here. Listen then, every one who hath been born of God doth not commit sin. What sin?, we ask. For if every sin is literally to be understood, the explanation will run contrary to that passage, 'if we say that we have no sin we deceive ourselves and the truth is not in us.' Let him then specify, what sin he means. Behold the entire drift and purpose of his circumlocution. Every one who is born of God sinneth not; because his seed remaineth in him.' He means the seed of God, that is the word of God.

Hence the Apostle says, I have begotten you through the Gospel. And he cannot sin because he hath been born of God. Let us then see in what we cannot sin: 'In this are manifested the sons of God, and the sons of the devil. Every one who is not righteous is not of God; and he who loveth not his brother.'

It is now clearly shown why he says, 'And he loveth not his brother.' Love alone constitutes the distinction between the sons of God and the sons of the devil. Let all sign themselves with the sign of the cross of Christ; let all answer, amen; let all say Hallelujah; let all be baptized; let all enter the Churches; let all build the walls of cathedrals; still the sons of God and the sons of the devil are only distinguishable from each other by charity. They who have charity have been born of God: they who have not charity have not been born of God' (*Augustine on the First Epistle of John*).

For the above quotation I am indebted to Faber's 'Primitive Doctrine of regeneration.'

5. 'From our creation we may look to our regeneration. If we be the sons of God we are renewed. And how shall it appear whether we be the sons of God? It is a golden rule: "Whosoever are led by the Spirit of God, they are the sons of God." If therefore you find your hearts unclean, your hands idle and unprofitable, your ways crooked and unholy, your corruptions alive and lively, never pretend to any renewing. You are the old man still' (*Bishop Hall's Sermons*, 1620).

'This our adoption is not a mere extrinsical denomination as is adoption amongst men; but is accompanied with a real change in those that are adopted, a new nature and spirit being infused into them, by reason of which as they are adopted to their inheritance in Christ, they are likewise begotten of God and born again to it by the supernatural work of regeneration. They are like their heavenly Father. They have His image renewed on their soul, and their Father's Spirit: they have it, and are acted and led by it.'

'We all pretend to be of the number of God's sons. Would we not study to cozen ourselves, the discovery whether we are or not would not be so hard. In many their false confidence is too evident. They have no appearance in them of the Spirit of God, not a footstep like his leading, nor any trace of that character, "As many as are led by the Spirit of God, they are the sons of God"; not a lineament of God's visage as their Father. "If ye know that He is righteous," says St. John, "ye know then that every one that doeth righteousness is born of him'" (*Archbishop Leighton on St. Peter*, 1660).

'They are much deceived in their opinions who think that they are faithful and regenerate, when that cannot be said concerning them which is said of the Colossians, "In the which ye also walked sometime when ye lived in them" – but rather, "Ye still walk in them and live in them'" (*Bishop Davenant*, 1627).

6. 'Never yet was there an instance of any that did vigorously to their utmost labour after grace, that did not also leave some good evidences behind them that they did obtain it: and certainly thou hast no reason to think that God will make thee the first instance and precedent' (*Bishop Hopkins*, 1670).

Chapter 4

1. John 1:13. John 3:3. John 3:5. John 3:7. John 3:8. Titus 3:5. 1 Peter 1:3. 1 Peter 1:23. James 1:18. 1 John 2:29. 1 John 3:9. 1 John 4:7. 1 John 5:1. 1 John 5:4. 1 John 5:18.

2. (1) 'In baptism those that come feignedly, and those that come unfeignedly, both be washed with the sacramental water, but both be not washed with the Holy Ghost, and clothed with Christ.'

'All that be washed with water be not washed with the Holy Spirit' (*Archbishop Cranmer*, 1553).

(2) 'Good and evil, clean and unclean, holy and profane, must needs pass by the sacrament of baptism, except you will indeed in more ample and large measure tie the grace of God unto it than ever did the Papists, and say that all be baptized be also saved' (*Archbishop Whitgift*, 1583).

(3) 'Are all they that are partakers of the outward washing of baptism, partakers also of the inward washing of the Spirit? Doth this sacrament seal up their spiritual ingrafting into Christ to all who externally receive it? Surely no! Though God hath ordained these outward means for the conveyance of grace to our souls, yet there is

no necessity that we should tie the working of God's Spirit to the sacraments more than to the word' (*Archbishop Usher*, 1624).

(4) 'In baptism, as the one part of that holy mystery is Christ's blood, so is the other part, the material water. Neither are these parts joined together in place, but in mystery; and therefore they be oftentimes severed, and the one is received without the other' (*Bishop Jewell*, 1559).

(5) 'Christ said, "Except a man be born again from above, he cannot see the kingdom of God." Ye must have a regeneration: and what is this regeneration? It is not to be christened in water as these firebrands (the Roman Catholics) expound it, and nothing else' (*Bishop Latimer*, 1540).

(6) 'Our hearers make use of sermons and discourses evangelical but to fill up void space of their time. The reason of this is a sad condemnation to such persons; they have not yet entertained the Spirit of God; they are in darkness; they are washed in water, but never baptized with the Spirit' (*Bishop Jeremy Taylor*, 1660).

(7) 'All receive not the grace of God which receive the sacraments of his grace' (Richard *Hooker*, 1597).

(8) 'Not all are regenerated who are washed with the baptismal water' (*Dr. Whitaker, Regius Professor of Divinity at Cambridge*, 1590).

3. 'Do thy beloved sins still lodge with thee and keep possession of thy heart? Then are thou still a stranger to Christ, and an enemy to God. The word and seals of life are dead to thee, and thou art still dead in the use of them all. Know you not that many have made shipwreck on the very rock of salvation? – that many who were baptized as well as you, and as constant attendants on all the worship and ordinances of God as you, yet have remained without Christ, and died in their sins, and are now past recovery? Oh! that you would be warned! There are still multitudes running headlong that same course tending to destruction, through the midst of all the means of salvation; the saddest of all to it, through word and sacraments, and all heavenly ordinances to be walking hellwards! Christians, and yet no Christians; baptized, and yet unbaptized! As the prophet takes in the profane multitude of God's own people with the nations, "Egypt and Edom;

all these nations are uncircumcised, and all the house of Israel are uncircumcised in heart"; thus, thus the most of us are unbaptized in heart' (*Archbishop Leighton*, 1680).

'Rastall's supposition is that all men, which are baptized with material water, are very Christian men, and have the true faith, and are those which Paul affirmeth to be without spot, blame or wrinkle. But thereto I say, nay; for even as the outward circumcision made not the Jews the elect people and children of salvation, so doth not the outward baptism make us the faithful members of Christ. But as they were the children of God who were inwardly circumcised, even so they that are washed inwardly from the concupiscence of this world are the members of Christ' (*John Frith, Reformer and Martyr*, 1550).

'As in the Old Testament the circumcision of the flesh profited the Jews nothing at all, without the circumcision of the Spirit, so likewise in the New Testament the baptism of water availeth nothing, without the baptism of the Spirit' (*Thomas Becon, Chaplain to Archbishop Cranmer*, 1553).

4. 'Grace sometimes precedes the sacrament, sometimes follows it, and sometimes does not even follow it' (*Theodoret*, 450).

'All did drink the same spiritual drink, but not with all was God well pleased; and when the sacraments were all common, the grace was not common to all, which constitutes the virtue of the sacraments. So also now, when faith is revealed which was then veiled, the layer of regeneration is common to all, who are baptized in the name of the Father, and of the Son, and of the Holy Ghost; but the grace itself of which they are sacraments, and by which the members of the body of Christ are regenerated with their Head, is not common to all' (*Augustine on the 77ᵗʰ Psalm*, 390).

'Outward baptism may be administered, where inward conversion of the heart is wanting: and on the other hand inward conversion of the heart may exist, where outward baptism has never been received' (*Augustine's Treatise on Baptism*, 390).

'Some have the outward sign, and not the inward grace. Some have the inward grace, and not the outward sign. We must not commit idolatry by deifying the outward element' (*Archbishop*

Usher, 1624).

'We must not glory because we are made partakers of the external sacrament, unless we obtain besides the internal and quickening work of Christ. For if this be wanting, as was said heretofore to Jews, "O ye uncircumcised in heart," so it may be justly said to us, "O ye unbaptized in heart" ' (*Bishop Davenant*, 1627).

'If outward baptism were a cause in itself possessed of that power either natural or supernatural, without the present operation whereof no such effect could possibly grow: it must then follow, that, seeing effects do never precede the necessary causes out of which they spring, no man could ever receive grace before baptism, which is apparently both known and also confessed to be otherwise in many particulars' (*Richard Hooker*, 1597).

5. 'The sacrament hath no grace included in it; but to those that receive it well, it is turned to grace. After that manner the water in baptism hath grace promised, and by that grace the Holy Spirit is given: not that grace is included in water, but that grace cometh by water' (*Bishop Ridley*, 1547).

'What is so common as water? What is so common as bread and wine? Yet Christ promiseth it to be found there, where he is sought with a faithful heart' (*Bishop Latimer*, 1540).

'That baptism hath a power, is clear, in that it is so expressly said "it doth save us". "What kind of power is equally clear from the way it is here expressed; not by a natural power of the element; though adapted and sacramentally used, it only can wash away the filth of the body; its physical efficacy or power reached no further: but it is in the hand of the Spirit of God as other sacraments are, and as the word itself is, to purify the conscience and convey grace and salvation to the soul, by the reference it hath to, and union with that which it represents. Sacraments are neither empty signs to them who believe, nor effectual causes of grace to them that believe not. Sacraments do not save all who partake of them, yet they do really and effectually save believers, for whose salvation they are means, as the other external ordinances of God do. Though they have not that grace which is peculiar to the author of them, yet a power they have such as befits their nature, and by reason of which they are truly said to sanctify and justify, and so to save, as the Apostle here avers of baptism' (*Archbishop Leighton*, 1680).

'Is Christ and the cleansing power of His blood only barely signified in the sacrament of baptism? Nay more. The inward things are really exhibited to the believer as well as the outward. There is that sacramental union between them that the one is conveyed and sealed up by the other. Hence are those phrases of being "born again of water and the Holy Ghost", etc. etc. The sacraments being rightly received do effect that which they do represent' (*Archbishop Usher*, 1624).

6. 'It is the received judgment of our Church that the faith of the parents, or of those that instead of the parents present the child in the congregation, is so far the infant's as to give him right unto the covenant' (*Archbishop Usher*, 1624).

7. 'Let us learn not to confide with Papists in the opus operatum, but inquire whether we possess all the other things, without which the inward effects of baptism are not secured' (*Bishop Davenant*, 1627).

'Many ignorant people among us, for want of better teaching, harbour in their minds such Popish conceits, especially that baptism doth confer grace upon all by the work done, for they commonly look no higher: and they conceive a kind of inherent virtue and Christendom, as they call it, necessarily infused into children, by having the water cast upon their faces' (*Archbishop Usher*, 1624).

'It is a pitiful thing to see the ignorance of the most professing Christianity, and partaking of the outward seals of it, yet not knowing what they mean; not appreciating the spiritual dignity and virtue of them. A confused fancy they have of some good in them, and this rising to the other extreme to a superstitious confidence in this simple performance and participation of them, as if that carried some inseparable virtue with it, which none could miss of, who are sprinkled with the water of baptism, and share in the element of bread and wine in the Lord's Supper' (*Archbishop Leighton*, 1680).

'Wicked is that Popish doctrine, that original sin is forgiven by baptism: and for all actual offences after baptism, partly by Christ's blood, and partly by our own satisfaction, we attain and get pardon of them' (*Bishop Babington, Bishop of Exeter*, 1594).

'Let us consider how corruptly the Church of Rome teacheth us touching this sacrament (baptism), and how horribly they have abused it. First they teach that baptism doth confer grace and wash away our sins ex opere operato, that is, even by the very washing only of the water, though there be no good motion of faith or belief in the heart of him that is baptized' (*Bishop Cooper*, 1570).

'The Papists maintain that grace is conferred upon little children in the sacrament of the New Testament, without faith or any good motive. This is to attribute a power to sacraments of themselves, and by a virtue of their own, in the case of little children: which we say is false. For we assert that grace is not conferred by the sacraments even upon little children from the work wrought, so that all necessarily have grace that receive the sacraments' (*Dr. Whitaker*, 1580).

8. 'If there be that cure that they speak of in the baptized, how is it that there is so little effect or token thereof? How is it that after baptism there remaineth so great crookedness and perverseness of nature, which we find to be no less than men from the beginning have complained of? How is it that it is so rare and hard a matter to be trained to goodness, and so easy and ready a matter to become nought?' (*Bishop Robert Abbot*, 1615).

'From those who are baptized in infancy subsequent faith is required; which if they exhibit not afterward, they retain only the outward sanctification of baptism, the inward effect of sanctification they have not' (*Bishop Davenant*, 1627).

'The true way of judging whether the Spirit of God be in us, is to consider our own debts. Righteousness and holiness are the only certain marks of regeneration' (*Bishop Sherlock*, 1740).

'As for those who are visibly reclaimed from a notorious wicked course, in them we likewise frequently see this change gradually made by strong impressions made upon their minds, most frequently by the word of God, sometimes by His providence, – till at length, by the grace of God, they come to a fixed purpose and resolution of forsaking their sins and turning to God, and after many strugglings and conflicts with their lusts, and the strong bias of their evil habits, this resolution, assisted by the grace of God, doth effectually prevail, and make a real change both in the temper of their minds, and course of their lives; and when this is done, and not before, they are said to be regenerate' (*Archbishop Tillotson*, 1691).

'The only certain proof of regeneration is victory' (*Bishop Wilson*, 1697).

9. It may be well to remark that this is also the doctrine of the Church of Scotland. 'The efficacy of baptism is not tied to that moment of time wherein it is administered; yet notwithstanding, by the *right use* of this ordinance, the grace promised is not only offered, but really exhibited and *conferred* by the Holy Ghost, to such (whether of age or infants), as that grace belongeth unto, according to the counsel of God's own will, in His appointed time' (*Scotch Confession of Faith, Chapter 28*).

10. 'There is in every sacrament a spiritual relation, or sacramental union between the sign and the thing signified; whence it comes to pass, that the names and effects of the one are attributed to the other' (*Scotch Confession of Faith. Chapter 27*).

11. 'What say you of infants baptized that are born in the Church? Doth the inward grace in their baptism always attend upon the outward sign? Surely, no. The sacrament of baptism is effectual in infants only to those and to all those who belong unto the election of grace. Which things, though we in the judgment of charity, do judge of every particular infant, yet we have no ground to judge so of all in general: or if we should judge so, yet it is not any judgment of certainty. We may be mistaken' (*Archbishop Usher*, 1620).

'All that receive baptism are called children of God, regenerate, justified: for to us they must be taken for such in charity, until they show themselves other. But the author, (Montague, a friend of Archbishop Laud) affirmeth that this is not left to men's charity, as you, saith he do inform the world, because we are taught in the service book of our Church earnestly to believe that Christ hath favourably received these infants that are baptized, that he hath embraced them with the arms of his mercy, that he hath given them the blessing of everlasting life; and out of that belief and persuasion we are to give thanks faithfully and devoutly for it. All this we receive and make no doubt of it: but when we have said all we must come to this, that all this is the charity of the Church, and what more can you make of it?' (*George Carleton, Bishop of Chichester,* 1619).

'We are to distinguish between the judgment of charity and the judgment of certainty. For although in the general we know that not every one that is baptized is justified or shall be saved, yet when we come to particulars, we are to judge of them that are baptized that they are regenerated and justified, and shall be saved until they shall discover themselves not to be such. And so our book of Common Prayer speaketh of them' (*George Downame, Bishop of Derry,* 1620).

'The office for baptizing infants carries on the supposition of an internal regeneration' (*Bishop Burnet,* 1689).

'There is justification for that prayer in our public liturgy, when the congregation gives thanks to God for the child baptized, that it hath pleased him to regenerate this infant by his Holy Spirit, etc. For it cannot be denied but that the holy ordinance of baptism, the seal of our sanctification doth take effect many times immediately in the infusion of present grace into the infant's soul, though many times also it hath not its effect till many years after. But seeing it is questionably true in many, we may and must charitably suppose it in every one, for when we come to particulars whom dare we exclude? And this we may do without tying the grace of regeneration necessarily to baptism, as some complain that we do' (*William Pemble, Magdalen Hall, Oxford,* 1635).

'The Apostles always, when they descend to particular men or Churches, PRESUME every Christian to be elect, sanctified, justified, and in the way of being glorified, until he himself shall have proved himself to be wicked, or an apostate' (*Bishop Davenant,* 1627).

'As to what he says, that no one can be a minister of the Church of England, who is not certainly persuaded of the regeneration of every infant baptized, neither also is that true. The minister truly gives God thanks after each infant has been baptized, that it has pleased God to regenerate him with his Holy Spirit. But it does not then follow that he ought to be certain of the regeneration of every infant baptized. For it is sufficient, if he is persuaded of the regeneration of some only, for instance, of elect infants, or if you like, even of some only of their number, that on that account he may be able, nay ought, to give God thanks for each and all baptized. Since who is elect he knows not: and it is but just that he should *by the judgment of charity presume*, that as many as be baptized are elect, – and if any are regenerated in baptism (which none but a Socinian or other Catabaptist will deny) regenerated' (*Dr. Durel, Dean of Windsor, and Chaplain to the King*, 1677).

12. 'The Catholic Church, which is the body of Christ indeed, consists of such as are truly sanctified and united to Christ by an internal alliance; so that no wicked person or unbeliever is a member of this body, solely by external profession of faith, and participation of the sacraments. We oppose this position to Bellarmine, who ventures to assert, that for any one to be called a member of the true Church no internal virtue is required, but only an external profession of faith and communion of the sacraments, and union with the Roman Church' (*Bishop Davenant*, 1627).

13. It was Archbishop Usher himself who proposed in 1634 that the English Articles should be received by the Irish Church. Yet he was the principal author of the Irish Articles of 1615. His biographer says, 'He very well understood the Articles of both Churches, and did then know that they were so far from being inconsistent or contradictory to each other, that he thought the Irish Articles did only contain the doctrine of the Church of England more fully' (*Life of Archbishop Usher, by Dr. Parr, his chaplain*, 1686).

14. 'It is a settled rule with casuists, that oaths are always to be taken in the sense of the imposers; the same is the case of solemn leagues or covenants. Without this principle no faith, trust, or mutual confidence could be kept up amongst men' (*Waterland on the Arian Subscriptions. Works, vol. 3. chap.* iii).

I take this opportunity of acknowledging my obligations for some of the quotations in this Tract, to two most valuable Books, Goode on 'The Effect of Infant Baptism', and 'The Voice of the Glorious Reformation' by the Rev. C. P. Miles.

That Man of Granite with the Heart of a Child

A new biography of J.C. Ryle

Eric Russell

"It is very good to have Ryle's story told afresh by some-one who understands it so well...Ryle was an Anglican to remember."

J. I. Packer

John Charles Ryle was born into a comfortable English family background – his father was a politician and businessman. Ryle was intelligent, a great sportsman (captain of cricket at Eton and Oxford), and was set for a career in his father's business, and then politics – a typical, well-to-do, 19th century family.

Then – disaster. The family awoke to find that their father's bank had failed, taking all the other businesses with it. Ryle had lost his job and his place in society.

Almost as a last resort, he was ordained into the ministry of the church. Who could have thought that such an uninspiring entry into the ministry could have such an impact on the spiritual life of a nation.

Ryle's reputation as a pastor and leader grew until he was appointed the first Bishop of Liverpool, a post he held for twenty years. He was an author who is still in print today (he put aside royalties to pay his father's debts) and a man once described by his successor as 'that man of granite with the heart of a child'. He changed the face of the English church.

ISBN 978-1-85792-631-6

Day By Day With J.C. Ryle:

A New daily devotional of Ryle's writings

J.C. Ryle

J.C. Ryle has become one of the most loved of British authors on church matters. He was the first Bishop of Liverpool, managing to establish a thriving diocese in that most sectarian of English cities. Although a convinced Evangelical he was regarded as fairminded with those who disagreed with him. Even Ryle's opponents in church politics wept when he died.

His books have remained in print for a hundred years because Ryle was able to touch the person in the street with clear teaching on doctrinal matters. He showed how the Bible was relevant.

His writings thus lend themselves to a devotional format and here is a new selection different to any that have gone before. Here Eric Russell (Ryle's biographer) has arranged writings according to themes that develop the reader's understanding on a topic before moving on to new pastures.

It is as refreshing as it is profound.

ISBN 978-1-85792-959-1

Christian Focus Publications

publishes books for all ages

Our mission statement –

STAYING FAITHFUL

In dependence upon God we seek to help make His infallible word, the Bible, relevant. Our aim is to ensure that the Lord Jesus Christ is presented as the only hope to obtain forgiveness of sin, live a useful life and look forward to heaven with Him.

REACHING OUT

Christ's last command requires us to reach out to our world with His gospel. We seek to help fulfill that by publishing books that point people towards Jesus and help them develop a Christ-like maturity. We aim to equip all levels of readers for life, work, ministry and mission.

Books in our adult range are published in three imprints.

Christian Focus contains popular works including biographies, commentaries, basic doctrine, and Christian living. Our children's books are also published in this imprint.

Mentor focuses on books written at a level suitable for Bible College and seminary students, pastors, and other serious readers. The imprint includes commentaries, doctrinal studies, examination of current issues, and church history.

Christian Heritage contains classic writings from the past.

Christian Focus Publications, Ltd
Geanies House, Fearn, Ross-shire,
IV20 1TW, Scotland, United Kingdom
info@christianfocus.com
www.christianfocus.com